Blood and Gifts

J. T. Rogers is the author of *The Overwhelming*, *Madagascar*, *White People*, *Murmuring in a Dead Tongue* and other plays. His works have been produced in London by the National Theatre, Tricycle Theatre and Theatre 503; toured the UK with Out of Joint; and been heard on BBC Radio. In New York City his plays have been seen at the Roundabout Theatre, the SPF Play Festival and commercially Off Broadway; they have also been staged in Australia, Canada, Israel, Germany and throughout the United States. His essays have appeared in *The Independent*, *New Statesman* and *American Theatre*. In New York City, Rogers is a resident playwright at New Dramatists and a member of the Dramatists Guild. He holds an honorary doctorate from the University of North Carolina School of the Arts.

J. T. ROGERS

Blood and Gifts

FARRAR, STRAUS AND GIROUX

NEW YORK

Farrar, Straus and Giroux
175 Varick Street, New York 10014

Originally published in 2010 by Faber and Faber Limited,
Great Britain
Published in the United States by Farrar, Straus and Giroux
First American edition, 2011

Library of Congress Control Number: 2011940266
ISBN: 978-0-86547-884-8

Our books may be purchased in bulk for promotional,
educational, or business use. Please contact your local bookseller
or the Macmillan Corporate and Premium Sales Department at
1-800-221-7945, extension 5442, or by e-mail at
MacmillanSpecialMarkets@macmillan.com.

www.fsgbooks.com
www.twitter.com/fsgbooks • www.facebook.com/fsgbooks

P1

For Rebecca, ever with me,
and Louisa, ever missed

Blood and Gifts was commissioned
by Lincoln Center Theater.

In the United States, the play was developed
at PlayPenn, in Philadelphia, and then further
at New Dramatists, in New York City.

Acknowledgements

I wish to thank the following people and organisations in both the US and UK for their editorial criticism, language translation, professional advice, or creative and financial support: Rebecca Ashley (as always); David Rogers, Lauren Sanders and Gus Reyes; Syed Abdul Rahim and Christian Parker; Marc Glick, Sue Charles, John Buzzetti and St John Donald; Paul Meshejian and everyone at the PlayPenn new play development conference in Philadelphia; the staff of New Dramatists, New York City; and André Bishop and all at Lincoln Center Theater.

Instrumental to the development of *Blood and Gifts* were the comments of Steve Coll, Jack Devine and Lawrence Wright. My thanks to all three for sharing their expertise.

The seed for this play was planted in 2008 when I was asked to contribute a short play to the Tricycle Theatre's twelve-play cycle of works about Afghanistan, *The Great Game*. My thanks to Jack Bradley for suggesting me for inclusion and to Rachel Grunwald and her cast for their excellent production.

Finally, I am grateful to Lucie Tiberghien and the actors with whom we workshopped this play together, first in Philadelphia and then in New York; to Nick Hytner, Sebastian Born and everyone at the National Theatre; and last but not least, to Howard Davies and our superb cast.

J. T. Rogers
London, 7 September 2010

Blood and Gifts had its U.S. premiere on November 21, 2011, at Lincoln Center Theater (André Bishop, Artistic Director; Bernard Gersten, Executive Producer) in the Mitzi Newhouse Theater, with the following cast (in order of appearance):

James Warnock Jeremy Davidson
Dmitri Gromov Michael Aronov
Colonel Afridi Gabriel Ruiz
Military Clerk Andrés Munar
Simon Craig Jefferson Mays
Abdullah Khan Bernard White
Saeed Pej Vahdat
Soldier Paul Niebanck
Administrative Aide Paul Niebanck
Political Speechwriter Andrew Weems
Congressional Staffer Liv Rooth
Walter Barnes John Procaccino
CIA Analyst Andrés Munar
Senator Jefferson Birch Robert Hogan
Other parts played by members of the Company

Director Bartlett Sher
Sets Michael Yeargan
Costumes Catherine Zuber
Lighting Donald Holder
Sound Peter John Still
Stage Manager Jennifer Rae Moore

Characters

in order of appearance

Dmitri Gromov
Russian, forties

James Warnock
American, thirties

Colonel Afridi
Pakistani, thirties

Military Clerk
a young Pakistani man

Simon Craig
English, late thirties

Abdullah Khan
Afghan, forties

Saeed
Afghan, twenties

Soldier
an American man, twenties or older

Two Mujahideen
Afghan men, twenties or older

Administrative Aide
an American man, twenties

Political Speechwriter
an American man, thirties

Congressional Staffer to Senator Birch
American, late twenties, female

Walter Barnes
American, fifties

CIA Analyst
an American man, twenties

Senator Jefferson Birch
American, fifties

The Ensemble
Airport travellers; Afghan refugees
and mujahideen; Pakistani pedestrians
and military personnel; guests at a Washington
fundraiser; celebrants and staff at the Irish and
American Embassies in Islamabad

Time and Place

1981 to 1991
Pakistan, America and Afghanistan

The physical engine of this play is to be found
in the rapidity and fluidity of its transitions.
Each scene flows into, or smashes against,
the next without pause

Author's Note

Lines in the play in Pashto, Farsi and Russian are written in the Roman alphabet for actors' ease of pronunciation.

The use of a slash (/) marks the point of overlapping dialogue.

A sentence ending with a dash (–) indicates that the speaker is cut off while talking.

A sentence that *ends* with an ellipsis (. . .) indicates the speaker has trailed off; one that *begins* with an ellipsis indicates a slight hesitation before the speaker begins.

Paragraph breaks mid-speech show where one thought ends and another commences.

BLOOD AND GIFTS

Whenever two people meet there are really
six people present. There is each man as he
sees himself, each man as the other person
sees him, and each man as he really is.

William James

The trouble with riding a tiger is that
eventually you will have to get off.

Winston Churchill

Act One

Pakistan. December 1981.
  The Islamabad Airport, early morning.
  *We hear the roar of a plane overhead and a flight
announcement – first in Urdu, then in English. Travellers
criss-cross the stage in a bustle of movement. Dmitri
Gromov, forties, stands reading a newspaper. Jim Warnock,
thirties, enters walking quickly, a small battered suitcase
in one hand and a diplomatic pouch under the other arm.
As Jim passes him, Gromov lowers his paper. His English
is good but his Russian accent is heavy.*

Gromov (*calling after him*) You are going wrong way.

  Jim realises he's talking to him, turns and stops.

Forgive me, but I could not help myself.
  (*Points.*) Airport exit is that direction.

Jim Thank you, but I'm meeting someone. I'm fine.

  As Jim starts to move again . . .

Gromov Ah! We have connection. I too am here to meet
someone. My wife arrives soon.

Jim Uh-huh.

Gromov The flight from Moscow.

Jim Uh-huh.

Gromov Summer heat here, it is too much for her. But
now that winter returns, she returns.

Jim I see.

Gromov Her flight delayed of course, but . . . (*He shrugs.*)
Pakistan is not Russia. What can one do?

Jim Well. Have a nice day.

As Jim turns . . .

Gromov Very impressive.

Jim Excuse me?

Gromov One suitcase and one pouch. To come to edge
of world with only this? Clearly, you are adventurous
man. When I first arrived here in Islamabad, I knew I
would be here for years. So I brought everything except –
what is saying? – kitchen sink.

Jim Forgive me, but I've got to –

Gromov Tell me, how long will *you* be here, comrade
James Warnock?

Neither man moves.
    *The other travellers have passed through and they
are alone now.*

Jim Too soon to tell.

Gromov And what brings you all the way to Pakistan?

Jim Work.

Gromov But of course. Man like yourself, you are here
to serve in your embassy. Officially.

Jim That's right.

Gromov And in what capacity will you be serving?

Jim I'm in education.

Gromov Again, connection! So am I. Officially.

Jim Good for you.
    It's been a pleasure. Give your wife my best.

4

Gromov And yours mine.

Jim stares at him.

Congratulations are in order. Just married, yes? Pity she is not going to join you. But perhaps your wife is not interested in education. Or perhaps, unlike you, she realises the danger such work can bring.

Jim My wife is none of your business.

Gromov I am only trying to –

Jim (*sharp, in Russian*) *Slooshayetye. Vy znayetye oo kavo ya rabotayoo, ee ya znayoo oo kavo vy rabotayetye, ee ya nye eemyeyoo vremenee dlya etova.* [Look. You know who I work for, I know who you work for, and I don't have time for this.]

The two men stare at each other.

Gromov I see. Then what *do* you have time for, comrade Warnock?

Jim You'll find out.

SCENE TWO

Islamabad. Afridi's office in the headquarters of the Inter-Services Intelligence Directorate (ISI), the Pakistani Army's intelligence branch, an hour later.

Afridi, thirties or older, stands in full military uniform. To his side is a spit-polished young Army Clerk taking the official minutes. Jim, suitcase by his side, hands Afridi the diplomatic pouch he carried at the airport.

Jim With my compliments, Colonel. And with high hopes for our work together.

Afridi opens the pouch and brings out a beautiful antique revolver.

Clerk (*to Afridi*) Oh, very nice, very good, very John Wayne, sir!

Afridi You are a generous man, Mr Warnock. How I wish your government shared your largesse.

(*Gesturing around the room.*) Tell me, where are the rest of you? Does your government think this struggle so unimportant that you alone will suffice?

Jim My government has sent me to start this operation *because* they think this struggle is so important. Now there may be only three of us here in Islamabad –

Afridi There are only three of you in all of Pakistan.

Jim I wish it were more, Colonel, but for now, yes, just three.

Afridi Then again, an hour ago there were only two of you. So perhaps what we should call *you*, Mr Warnock, is 'progress'.

Clerk Oh, very nice, very good, very Noël Coward, sir!

Afridi (*inspecting the gun*) Do you know what I admire most about your country, Mr Warnock? Arizona. The deserts there stop one's heart.

A rumpled Simon Craig, late thirties, enters in a rush.

Simon Sorry, sorry.

Afridi Mr Craig, late as always.

Simon Traffic. Rickshaw, water buffalo: God knows. (*To Jim, extending his hand.*) Ah! You must be –

Afridi points the pistol at Simon.

(*Freezing.*) Hell–o.

Afridi Have *you* been to Arizona, Mr Craig?

Simon Can't say I have, Colonel.

Afridi You English have no deserts. This is why you are such a weak and soft people. If even part of your country were hard and dry – (*gesturing to Jim*) like his – you would not have lost your grip on this part of the world. Then again, if you had not, I would not even be allowed in this room. Would I? So perhaps I should be grateful that God has made your little island so lush.

He puts the pistol down and slaps his hands together.

So.

The men are all business now.

Jim You'll have a hundred thousand rifles by the end of the month. 303s. Greek and Indian, Egyptian guns to follow.

Simon As for the Chinese –

Jim (*to Simon*) You've confirmed?

Simon They're kicking in munitions. Ancient stuff, but it'll work with the Egyptian weapons.
My God, Russian soldiers being shot with Chinese bullets. Sometimes the world is so beautiful.

Afridi And what else?

Jim Nothing else. For now that's all I'm / authorised to hand over.

Afridi I'm sorry . . . I'm sorry . . . I am confused. I thought you were sent here because your government wanted to win.

Jim With all due respect, this isn't a football game.

Afridi With all due respect, we play cricket here.

Simon Perhaps we should focus on / how we plan to . . .

Afridi These weapons are an insult.

Jim I understand your frustration, but –

Afridi Russian tanks are two hundred and fifty kilometres from Islamabad. From the chair you are sitting in.

Jim And I'm here to make sure they don't come any closer.

Afridi And what of the men who are *already* doing that? They are to fight the Soviet Army with bolt-action rifles? For two years those Afghans have been freezing in their mountains, fighting for you and me, Mr Warnock. So forgive me if your 'gift' does not impress.

Jim Look, as station chief I will work day and night. But I answer to those above me, Colonel, and they say deniability, first and foremost. No weapons that can be traced to us.

Now we'd like the majority of these rifles to go to –

Simon Ahmed Shah Massoud.

Afridi No.

The two men stare at Afridi.

Simon Why not? He and his men are banging away at the Soviets.

Afridi Because Massoud is a Tajik. Most Afghans are Pashtun and they see Tajiks as spies for the Iranians. We must focus our support on a Pashtun commander.

Jim Who do you suggest?

Afridi Gulbuddin Hekmatyar. He is here in Pakistan training an army of fellow Afghan mujahideen. The 'Army of Sacrifice', ready to sacrifice all.

Simon Well that's smashing, but we're going to want to spread *some* of these weapons around to other warlords. Our intelligence shows this will / be much more effective.

Afridi *Your* intelligence? You were *born* there? I did not realise Manchester was a suburb of Kabul.

Gentlemen, those of us who serve in the ISI, we know who is who and what is what here. My agency's intelligence will be the basis of our strategy.

I went personally to the seven main Afghan commanders. I said to each, 'Of course, *you* are the most powerful. *You* and your forces are whom the Russians fear most. But tell me, *after* you, which commander is number two?' All said: Hekmatyar. So, yes, we will give them each some support, but Hekmatyar will be the point of our spear.

Because *we* select who gets weapons. This is our agreement, yes?

Jim Yes.

Afridi And throughout this operation you will go through me and no one else.

Jim Agreed.

Afridi And you will have no contact, in person or in any other form, with anyone in the Afghan resistance.

Simon Well, that's ridiculous.
(*To Jim.*) Was that part of your agreement?

Jim ISI is running this operation, not us.

Simon Are you actually / going to . . .

Jim What he says goes. / Those are my orders.

Simon Bollocks!
(*To Afridi.*) Colonel, I understand we're the third party here, 'facilitating' and all that, but the British government is not going to be part of a covert war where we're not even allowed to talk to those we're supporting!

Afridi Mr Craig, are you a Jew?

Simon stares at him.

My sources tell me you are a Jew. Is this true?

Simon . . . Yes, actually.

Afridi I am a Jew too.

Simon . . . I see.

Afridi Not a true Jew.

Simon No.

Afridi But like a Jew.

Simon Right.
    What *are* you talking about?

Afridi Pakistan is the Israel of this region. A nation surrounded by enemies on all sides. Russia, Iran, Hindustan. Pushing against us, seeking to drive us into *our* Sea of Galilee. Like your people, we do not have the luxury of trusting others. Our fate will be held in our hands. Ours alone.
    Thank you, gentlemen.

Jim It's been a pleasure.

Simon Yes, truly enlightening.

Jim Colonel, I'd be grateful if we could get together again soon and talk further about the challenges we're all facing here.

Afridi Somewhere other than here you mean.

Jim Wherever you'd like. As my guest, of course.

Afridi Perhaps we could have lunch.

Jim That'd be terrific.

Afridi A little chicken, bottle of wine.

Jim Absolutely. If that's what / you'd like to do.

Afridi And then you could start asking me questions. Little questions, so simple to answer. Answers for which you will be willing to pay. And all of a sudden, with the chicken and the wine, I would be working for you. Another man in your pocket, another set of eyes in your head.

We will only meet here and only when we must. This is not friendship, Mr Warnock, this is business. Only.

SCENE THREE

Jim and Simon on the street in Islamabad, moments later.

Simon Well, that was fruitful. You got a lesson in cultural sensitivity and I got a rabbi.

Jim It's Simon, right?

Simon Yes. Pleasure. James, is it?

Jim Jim.

Simon Christ, you must be knackered. Let me drop you off at your flat.

Jim No, I'm fine.
Simon, I'm going down to Peshawar.

Simon You mean, *now*?

Jim Yeah.

Simon Don't you want to at least – I don't know – cold beer, sleep?

Jim I'm fine.
Look, officially I'm going to get a look at the Afghani refugee camps / on the border, but . . .

Simon Afghan.

Jim Sorry?

Simon Afghan is the person. Afghani is the money.

Jim Thank you.

Simon I only, because I made the mistake when I first got here. While I was wooing a contact. He was incensed. Set me back months. Still calls me 'Pound Sterling' just to keep sticking the knife in.

So look, from Peshawar, the best way to get to Kabul is to –

Jim Kabul's irrelevant. Russians are everywhere. Starting today we're going to run everything out of Pakistan. Here and Peshawar, where we'll be closer to the border.

Simon Yes, but when you do need to cross into Afghanistan –

Jim I can't cross over.

Simon Oh, it's nothing. Done it for years. I'll show you the best / way to . . .

Jim I'm not allowed to, Simon.

Simon . . . Really? When did this –

Jim New rules. Now that we're up and running, headquarters wants no more US operatives on Afghan soil.

Simon Of course. If the Russians caught you –

Jim I'm more worried about local actors.

Simon Right. Is that who got ahold of your man here before you?

Jim Yeah.

Simon What *did* happen to him?

Jim He got slit open, chin to navel. I promised my wife I wouldn't end up like that.

Simon Oh! Me, too. Well, the wife part. Just recently, actually. Jemma.

Jim Congratulations.

Simon Thank you. Yes, life is full of surprises. How long have you . . .?

Jim Just last month.

Simon Really! Where did you honeymoon?

Jim This is it.

Simon Ah. Well. That's very . . . something of you.

Jim I need my own asset, Simon.
   If we're gonna have any chance of success here, I need someone in Afghanistan I can run operations through without getting a permission slip from the ISI.

Simon . . . I see. So what you said in there was total –

Jim Exactly.

Simon Well played.
   What are you looking for?

Jim Someone Pashtun, based in the border region.

Simon Of course. Perfect sense.

Jim And really fighting the Soviets. I don't want one of these warlords who talks a good game but spends all his time screwing his mistress in Dubai.

Simon Well, that narrows things considerably.

Jim Who I can trust. Build up without worrying he's gonna switch sides and start using our weapons on us.

Simon Christ, what a nightmare that would be.

Well. There's only one man fits the bill. He's as close as any of these warlords come to a secularist. Fierce, effective; solid as a rock.

Jim When can I meet him?

Simon Well, that depends.

Jim On what?

Simon On what you're giving me in return.

Jim You mean other than trying to stop the Soviets from winning the Cold War?

Simon Indeed I do.

Jim Something other than furthering the special relationship / between our two countries?

Simon Oh, don't – don't even start. 'The special relationship'? Are you serious? Do you know what 'the special relationship' means on our end? We bend over and you give it to us special.

Jim Simon, I'm just –

Simon How'd you get here this morning?

Jim What do you –

Simon Transportation. Here.

Jim Car.

Simon Driver?

Jim Yeah.

Simon Air-conditioning?

Jim Yeah.

Simon Bastard. Do you know why I was late this morning? To the meeting *I* set up? Because I drove. Myself. I am the only white man in Islamabad who has to drive himself.

That's how cheap Her Majesty is. And we're not *just* cheap, mind you. Oh, no. We're cheap *and* obvious. My office – *in* the British Embassy – has a sign on the door that reads: 'Regional Diplomatic Officer'. I mean, how much more fucking obvious can they make me? Why don't they just write: 'MI6: Do. Not. Talk. To. Me.'

Jim So what do you want?

Simon In. On everything.
    Look, you've been sent here so – clearly – things are about to heat up. You've got the chequebook, you're running the show now, fine. Now I may not have a pot to piss in but I know this area. Back of my hand. The Afghans are charming, semi-civilised, and utterly untrustworthy. They are the French without the food. I know who to go to, who not to go to. You will *need* that / kind of support.

Jim Fine.

Simon . . . So, you mean . . . what by that?

Jim In the loop. Seat at the table. You've got my word.

Simon Right. Good.
    (*Then:*) Sorry, but I need to ask – just this once, I promise – your word.

Jim Yes?

Simon Is it any good?
    Because I'm not them. Just so we're clear.

SCENE FOUR

A safe house in the mountains of the Frontier Province of Pakistan, near the border with Afghanistan, the next evening. Bitterly cold.

On one side of the room sits Jim. Behind him and off to the side stands a young American Soldier, holding a US military-issue assault rifle. Between the two men lies Jim's suitcase. Across from them are two Afghans. Abdullah Khan, forties, sits facing Jim. To his side stands Saeed, twenties, an old battered bolt-action rifle slung over his shoulder.

On the floor in the middle of the room are two teacups and a cassette player. All four men stare at it as it plays Rod Stewart's 'Da Ya Think I'm Sexy?'

No one moves.

Abdullah gestures to Saeed, who steps forward, punches the off button, then steps back. Abdullah speaks in very rough, broken English, his accent thick as he seeks the right words.

Abdullah My son love this music. This music hurt my heart.
(*He shrugs.*) But this what children for.

Jim So they tell me.

Abdullah You, no son?

Jim No, not yet.

Abdullah But, you wish for?

Jim Yes I do. Very much.

Abdullah A son . . . eh . . . a son . . .
(*Struggling, he switches to Pashto.*) Zoy da Allah la loree yawa dalay da. Da doy Lapara mozh jangezho aw ham mroo. [A son is a gift from God. They are whom we fight and die for in the end.]

Without moving, Saeed translates. He is far more fluent, but his accent is also thick.

Saeed He says sons are God's gift. He says in the end, we live and we fight only for them.

16

Abdullah (*to Saeed, sharply*) *Saeeda! Za chi sa wayam hagha waya!* [Saeed! When you speak as me, speak exactly as me.]

Saeed *Balay saab.* [Yes, sir.]

Abdullah (*to Jim*) I no – (*gestures to his mouth*) English good. But I – (*his ears*) very good.

Jim And I will learn your language. To show my respect and commitment.

    Abdullah points at the cassette player.

Abdullah This, Shuravi.

Saeed (*to Jim*) This is our word for 'Soviet'. We took this from their –

Abdullah (*to Saeed*) *Day pohezhee!* [He knows!]
    (*To Jim.*) Shuravi soldier love this music too. All carry this mash-een. So we – (*gestures*) bomb, inside. Two year, we – (*the same gesture*) bomb. Shuravi pen, watch, thermos.

Jim Your success in fighting the Shuravi and their Afghan army is well known.

Abdullah *Koom Afghan pawtz?* [What Afghan army?]

Saeed (*translating*) 'What Afghan army?'

Abdullah *Sthaa matlab, 'Da Afghanistan Razakaar Pawtz'?*

Saeed 'You mean this – "Volunteer Army of Afghanistan"?'

Abdullah *Shuravayan chi da tupak pa zaur pa yu Afghan, askari kawi / nau da Afghan raza kar na dai.*

Saeed 'When the Shuravi put a gun to a man's head, he is not volunteering.'

Abdullah (*to Saeed*) *Day pooh ka.* [Make him understand.]

Saeed These godless Shuravi try and force Afghan to kill Afghan. But we will not fight our brothers.

Abdullah (*to Jim*) *Hets kala na!* [Never!]

Saeed Only the Shuravi are our enemy. Our eyes are fixed on them!

The sound of mortar fire in the distance.

Soldier (*to Jim*) Sir. We need to –

Without looking at him, Jim gestures to the Soldier to stop talking.

Abdullah I sorry this tea poor.

Jim It was fine. Thank you.

Abdullah Here, Pakistan? Tea?
(*He makes a face, and in Pashto:*) *Bay kara chai di.* [Terrible.]
(*Pointing.*) One day you cross border. Then you . . . (*Mimes drinking.*) Afghan tea. Then, *beyaa ba tha pooh say.* [You will know.]

Jim One day I will.

Abdullah For us, tea, life. Not have tea, not Afghan. But you know who first bring tea us?

Jim With all due respect, we need to –

Abdullah Russian. Hundred year go. *First* time try conquer. Just as now, they, eh . . . (*Searching for the word.*) soak land. Blood. (*Pointing at the teacups.*) But, leave gift. In blood, in death, still, gift.

The sound of mortar fire, this time a little closer.

Soldier Sir, we do not have clearance to be here this long.

Jim (*without looking at him*) I understand.

Soldier My orders are to get you back to Peshawar before –

Jim (*silencing him*) I understand.
   (*To Abdullah.*) I have come into the mountains because our peoples share a common enemy. I wish to help you against that enemy. But to do so, I need a man I can trust, who will trust me. Someone based over there in Afghanistan who –

Saeed Will be your ears and eyes.

Jim Yes.

Saeed But you have satellite and spaceship. These are better than Pashtun ears and eyes.

Jim I need someone on the ground, and I can't set foot in your country.

Saeed You are CIA, you step where you wish.

Jim Would that were so.

Saeed And in return for our ears and eyes?

Jim I will help you.

Saeed How?

Jim Every way I can.

   Saeed and Abdullah look at each other, then back at Jim.

Abdullah I, man, honour.

Jim This is what I hear.

Abdullah I show respect. You ask, we come.

Jim And for this I / am grateful.

Abdullah We cross border, meet you. Cross landmine, risk life, meet you. So . . .

(He leans in and switches to Pashto.) Ka thaasee zmozh sara da shaatho pa hakla khabaree kaway, thaasee baayad pa khwala ke shaath walarai.

Saeed *(translating)* 'If you wish to speak to us of honey, you should have honey in your mouth.'

Jim and Abdullah stare at each other.

Jim Fair enough.

Jim puts his suitcase in the middle of the room. Saeed crosses to it and opens it. We see that it is stuffed with American dollars.

(To Abdullah.) This will be a monthly gift. But anything you get from us does not come from us. You and I have not met, this meeting never happened.

Saeed *(gesturing to the money)* And for this you want –

Jim Information. On the ISI.

Abdullah and Saeed look at each other, then back to Jim as he continues.

Weapons, money: what they're doing with them, who they're giving them to. How big are the arms shipments they're moving through the Khyber Pass. What's exactly *in* those arms shipments. Which commanders are getting cash, which are not. Every operation they run in your country, I need to know. And if you give me what I need . . . *(He points to the suitcase.)* I'll give you what you need. One hand washes the other.

Saeed Here we do not waste precious water on our hands.

Jim I'm saying –

Saeed That we should spy on our Pakistani brothers who back our struggle.

Jim With all due respect, your struggle needs all the help it can get.

(*To Abdullah.*) This is not about buying your loyalty. This is about a long-term commitment, to you. No other commander, just you. And if you work with me and no one knows, you will find that my support will take you very far.

Abdullah and Saeed look at each other. Abdullah nods.

Saeed (*pointing to the suitcase*) This gift we will take.

Jim Then the first thing we need to do is –

Saeed But this is not enough.

(*Holding up his rifle.*) This is the rifle of my grandfather. This is what we fight with against the greatest army in the world.

Bring us weapons and we will give you what you need.

Jim (*pointing to the suitcase*) This is what I've brought. This is my offer.

Saeed (*to Abdullah*) *Ayaa day pa day hakla jedee day?* [Is he serious with this?]

Abdullah *Saeeda! Day praizhda, che khpala khabara / pora kee.* [Saeed! Let him finish what he / has to say.]

Jim I can also get you radio equipment.

Saeed (*pointing at the cassette player*) If we wish for music we have this!

Jim (*to Abdullah*) I will get you medical supplies, better clothes so your men don't freeze to death / this winter.

Abdullah This coat my father! This only clothe ever need!

Jim I am offering you my help.

Saeed You are offering us Band-Aids and dirty green paper!

Jim (*to Saeed*) You want more? Show me results.
(*To Abdullah.*) If you get me information, then I will also get you weapons.

Saeed We don't need weapons then, we need them now!
(*Pointing at the Soldier's gun.*) / Those are what we need! So give us those!

Jim Are you listening to what I'm telling you? / Are you hearing anything that I am saying?

Soldier Sir! We cannot be here any longer!

Abdullah raises his hand and there is silence.

Abdullah You say you want support our people.

Jim Yes.

Abdullah Help our people.

Jim Yes, I do.

Abdullah Then why you support wolf with face of man? Why you support enemy, *all* Afghan?

Jim . . . I don't – (*To Saeed.*) Who is he talking about?

Abdullah (*spitting out the name*) Gulbuddin Hekmatyar.
(*To Saeed.*) *Wartha wowaaya!* [Tell him!]

Saeed Hekmatyar is fanatic! He throw acid at woman, only for not covering face!

Abdullah I know this man! Twenty year, I know him!

Saeed Hekmatyar fight for his idea of God only. If you do not believe in his idea of Islam, you must die!

Abdullah This not right. Our war not for God, our war for Afghanistan! I fight for *all* my people! *All* / my country!

22

Jim (*to Abdullah*) Hekmatyar is a commander, you are a commander, and you are both fighting / the Shuravi.

Abdullah Where from?

Jim I came straight from Peshawar to these mountains / to meet you.

Abdullah No! You – (*Jabbing his finger at Jim.*) Where *you* from?

Jim I'm from Cleveland.

Abdullah (*to Saeed*) *Mathlab yeah sa dai?* [What does he mean?]

Saeed *Day Clevelandstani.* [He is from Cleveland.]

Abdullah Ah! Yes, I know!
(*Then, jabbing his finger at himself:*) I, Nuristani. I, *Khan*, Nuristan.

Saeed He is the eldest son of the eldest son of a khan of Nuristan. This is who *he* is!

Abdullah Hekmatyar? (*He spits on the ground.*)

Saeed He is from Kunduz. We Pashtun have no history in Kunduz. A man without history cannot lead!

Jim Be that as it may, he and his army are part of / the same struggle.

Saeed He and his army do nothing for our people! We are over there in our country fighting and dying, but never once does Hekmatyar bring his army out of Pakistan!

Abdullah But this wolf, you give weapon! This wolf, / you arm!

Jim Look! If he's getting weapons it's from Pakistani intelligence, not us.

Saeed You think we are children? The ISI supports who you wish! Hekmatyar would have nothing without your blessing!

Jim (*to Abdullah*) With all due respect, I have not slept in seventy-two hours. I have been waiting / for you in this icebox for over . . .

Saeed You stand there and ask us to spy on our Pakistani brothers? 'This hand washes that'? Our hands are clean! Give us weapons, not lies!

Jim You think you're going to get a better offer than this? From who?
(*Pointing to the suitcase.*) This, or nothing! You will get nowhere against the Russians without us! You *need* us!

Saeed erupts, moving toward Jim.

Saeed We do not need you, we need your weapons! Give us what you give Hekmatyar! / Give us honour! Give us justice!

Abdullah (*restraining*) *Saeeda, bus! / Domra kafee dee! Tha deer leree zay! Mozh na so kawlaay chee* . . . [That is enough, Saeed! / You are going too far! We cannot . . .]

Soldier (*gripping his rifle*) Sir! . . . Sir! . . . SIR!

Jim rises to his feet, cutting over the cacophony.

Jim Allahu Akbar!

He stands with his arms raised high over his head as the others stare.

Allahu Akbar! (*He lowers his arms.*)
That's what they're shouting, right now, from the rooftops of Kabul. Your people, pushing back against the Shuravi, fighting to make a difference.

I don't care about Hekmatyar. What he gets, does: unimportant. The question is, are *you* going to be important?

I *fought* for this assignment – left my life, my *wife* – because here, right now, I have a chance – *we* have a chance – to do what is right.

He steps toward Abdullah and extends his hand.

Join me and you have my word: whatever it takes, I will do. And we *will* make a difference.

SCENE FIVE

A refugee camp in Peshawar, near the border with Afghanistan, the next morning.
Amidst an excited crowd of Afghans, Gromov and Jim watch a sporting event.

Gromov (*pointing before them*) Buzkashi. The refugees, this is their favourite pastime. Back in Afghanistan they are wild for it.

Jim (*leaning in*) What is that they're throwing?

Gromov Ah! You must be careful, comrade. The horse riders will not slow down. If man leans in at wrong time when watching buzkashi . . . (*Shrugs.*) It would grieve me to see that happen to you.

Jim I'm sure it would. Very thoughtful of you.

Gromov (*pointing in front of them*) They throw goat carcass. The object of buzkashi is to reach down from galloping horse, grab goat, fight off other men, and toss carcass on earth at prescribed location.

Jim Somehow I don't think it's going to catch on back home.

Gromov It is deceiving sport. When you first watch, your eyes are always on rider. But in truth, horse is secret to victory. The rider with best support, he is victor. Always.

Forgive me, but I must say something, comrade Warnock. You look terrible.

Jim Thank you.

Gromov At pace you are going, you will burn self out. You have been in Pakistan – what? – less than two days and nights. And already you have come from Islamabad here to Peshawar, from Peshawar to . . . Where *did* you go last night, comrade?

Jim I've just been here.

Gromov With the refugees.

Jim Where else would I go?

Gromov Where indeed.

This country never ceases to amaze me. Look at us. Two days, two encounters. At this rate we will soon be inseparable. Like Stalin and Roosevelt. Or better yet, you will be Sonny and I will be Cher.

Jim You might want to run that by your wife first.

Gromov Alas, she did not make yesterday's flight.

Jim What a surprise.

Gromov Our daughter Masha is very sick.

Jim . . . I'm sorry to hear that.

Gromov She has pain in stomach. Enough to make her cry out. For body to shake. My wife will stay with her back in Moscow until she is better.

Jim But then who will –?

Gromov My mother raises our daughter. Old, old woman raising young headstrong girl? Trust me: never good idea.

(*Gestures to the refugees around them.*) You see, comrade, my entire family sacrifices for these people. But you know all about sacrifice from your time in Iran, yes?

Jim stares at him.

It has been – what? – only two years since your shah fell and those fanatics took power. For someone like you who was there when this happened, the wounds must be very fresh.

Jim You've got the wrong fellow, comrade. I've never been to Iran.

Gromov We knew once your shah fell, you and yours would look to expand your influence in this region. But Afghanistan? Whose bright idea was that? Nothing but dust and earth. It is like your Texas. Why would you want another Texas? Ah! I have proposition. We give you Afghanistan, you give us Texas. Then we will all be unhappy in new ways and everything will be good.

Jim Tempting, but we'll pass.

Gromov But tell me, comrade, when men of Tehran went in blink of eye from suits and clean faces to smocks and beards, calling for martyrdom, did you not feel personally responsible? Knowing such rivers of blood would never have spilled if you had not blindly supported that despot / until it was too late.

Jim I told you, I've never been in Iran.

Gromov (*in Farsi*) *Bash, bash. Barasthi shuma azam dashthi / dar har chiz dakhil na bashed. Aya shuma sababi ghalati yehb mathawaqif sakhtani an anasur khashamgin az . . .* [Come, come. Are you really going to pretend that

27

you were / not there in the midst of everything? That you were not instrumental in the failure to stop those madmen from . . .]

Jim What is that? What are you – is that – what – is that Farsi? I don't speak Farsi . . . I don't know what you're saying . . . *I don't know what you're saying.*

As Jim rises to leave . . .

Gromov Comrade, game is still playing!

Jim You told me you had something you needed me to see.

Gromov (*pointing to the game*) And here it is. You must understand / significance of this.

Jim I'm a busy man, Mr Gromov. And if you'll allow me, maybe you and yours would be running things a little better in Kabul if you spent less time watching goat tossing and more time dealing with the fact the Afghans want to slit your soldiers' throats.

Gromov And how would you know this, comrade? Have you been to Kabul? Have you seen Afghanistan with your own eyes?

Jim I've got plenty of eyes telling me / what I need to know.

Gromov (*pointing to the field*) *This* is Afghanistan. Savagery, chaos. *This* is what you need to understand. You think we were eager to step into this? Their government asked our army to come. We are there by invitation of the / People's Democratic Party of Afghanistan.

Jim Right . . . right . . . and when your tanks rolled across the border, did your boys find a lot of cheering? When they started killing people in Kabul left and right, was that part of the invitation?

Gromov We liberated Kabul! We are binding those tribes / into a country!

Jim Spare me your government-approved / boilerplate, comrade!

Gromov I am not speaking as government! I am speaking as man! I see that medieval country! I see lives of their children! Girls, age my Masha, sold, raped, killed! I am to see this and do nothing? What kind of father would –

He stops as they both realise they are drawing attention to themselves. They stare straight ahead, voices lowered.

Jim Why the hell are you telling me this?

Gromov Because no one is talking.

Jim turns and looks at him.

Above us, no one. Washington, Moscow: your side does not speak to mine, nor mine to yours.
You are new, comrade. Here, this is very rare. So your arrival is opportunity.
For you, this is proxy war, yes? But if our sides are not talking, the rules will change. Escalation. Then your army will come here too. Your army fighting our army? Can you imagine *those* rivers of blood?

Jim . . . All right.
But only like this, out in public where people can see us.

Gromov Of course. We would not want our people to think we are meeting private.

Jim No, we would not.

Gromov Then how would your people know they could trust you?

Jim Or yours you.

Gromov Interesting, yes? We dedicate, we sacrifice, yet still, so little trust.

We are both husbands, comrade, far from home. Here, we are both sacrificing. This is common bond, yes? Let us build on this. For both our sides, you and I, we must find way to trust.

The two men stare at each other.

Jim Abdur Rahman.

Gromov . . . I do not know what you / are saying.

Jim The last true King of Afghanistan.

Do you know what he said on his deathbed, comrade? What he whispered in the ear of his son and successor?

(*Leaning in.*) 'Never trust the Russians.'

SCENE SIX

July 1983. Two years later.

The Frontier Province of Pakistan, near Jalalabad. Afternoon. Blazing hot.

Jim and Saeed stand before a large company of men – mujahideen all armed with brand new rifles. Jim watches as Saeed drills the men. He barks at the men and they roar back as one.

Saeed *Thayar sai!* [Get ready!]

The Men *Zuwand! Zuwand!* [Life! Life!]

The call-and-response builds to a climax. Then Jim steps forward.

Jim (*to the men*) Now listen up, all of you.

(*He holds up one of the rifles; then to the men in one breath.*) As a representative of the government of the United States I am duty bound to inform you that these sniper rifles are not to be used in any way, shape or form for assassinations; these sniper rifles, that come equipped with night-vision scopes and can shoot a Shuravi officer in the head from a mile away, are for the battlefield only; once these weapons leave my hands I have no ability to control what you do with them or how you use them; but, I repeat, these weapons are for the battlefield and not to be used to kill Shuravi officers above the rank of captain in or around Jalalabad under the cover of darkness.

(*To Saeed.*) All yours.

As Jim turns away . . .

Saeed Warnock saab.

Jim Yeah?

Saeed What did you just say?

Jim What do you think I just said?

Saeed I have no idea.

Jim Good.

Saeed But what do I tell them?

Jim Tell them what these weapons are for and that I have said all I need to say.

Saeed (*trying to understand*) So, these rifles are designed to sniper Shuravi?

Jim I didn't say that.

Saeed But you just –

Jim I don't know what you're talking about.

Saeed You told us how to –

Jim Saeed, listen to me!
I cannot know. Anything. Ever.

The deafening roar of a warplane overhead. The men thrust their guns at the sky.

Don't shoot! Don't shoot!

The men lower their weapons as the plane flies on. No one moves, listening. Then . . .

It's all right. That far up, they didn't see us.

The men have circled around Jim and Saeed.

Saeed, I can't wait for the Khana any longer. I've got to get back to Peshawar before dark.

Mujahid One (*to Saeed*) *Poshtana zani waka.* [Ask him.]

Mujahid Two *Wu, waa ya ka.* [Yes, do it.]

Saeed Warnock saab . . . we have question.

Mujahid One *Zar kawa!* [Hurry up!]

Mujahid Two *Makhki thar day chi komandan / dalta rasi!* [Before the commander / gets here!]

Saeed (*silencing them*) *Sama da!* [All right!]
(*To Jim.*) Private question. Just us. No one else, yes?

The men all stare at Jim.

Jim Okay.

Saeed (*leaning in . . .*) Who is Colitas?

Jim Who?

Saeed Your Colitas, who is she?
We hear her, think of her, before each battle.

Mujahid One (*in rough English*) Colitas!

Mujahid Two (*as well*) Yes!

Saeed What does she look like? Tell us.

Mujahid Two Yes!

Saeed and the Men stare intently at Jim. He stares back at them.

Jim I have no idea what you're talking about.

Saeed Colitas! You know her! All American know her!

He leans in and begins to reverently sing the opening lyrics to The Eagles' 'Hotel California'. The men join in. As they all build in volume and intensity . . .

Jim Yeah . . . Yeah . . . Okay . . . (*Stopping them.*) Okay.

Saeed and the Men stare at him in anticipation.

Uh, no. Not a woman. 'Colitas' . . . it's, uh . . . (*He mimes smoking a joint.*)

Saeed What is . . . ? (*He mimics the gesture.*)

Jim Pot . . . marijuana.

Saeed Drugs?

Jim Yeah.

Saeed 'Colitas' is drugs?

Jim Yeah.

Saeed We sing song of drugs?

Jim Yeah.

Saeed (*to his men*) *Day waayee 'Colitas' yu nasha da.* [He says 'Colitas' means 'drugs'.]

The men wail in shock and despair.

Mujahid One / *Da sanga kadalay si?* [How can this be?]

Mujahid Two *Khuda ba muz tha par day saza ra ki!* [God will strike us for this!]

Saeed (*to Jim*) This is a dark day.

Abdullah appears.

Abdullah (*roaring at his men*) *Ma thaasi da thuri da para ruzali yast!* [I have trained you for swords, not for singing!]
    (*He gestures to their rifles.*) *Na da sanduru da para!* [Your heart should be full of those!]

Saeed *Khu muz yawazi doona* – [But we were only –]

Abdullah *Saeeda! Khpal kasan di waruza!* [Saeed! Train your men!]

Saeed *Bali saab!* [Yes, sir!]

The men scramble back to their weapons as Abdullah approaches Jim.

Jim Salaam alaikum, Abdullah khana.

Abdullah Alaikum salaam, Warnock khana.
    (*Gesturing to his men.*) All of them, always, this music. Singing, tape recording. Poison in my ears!

Jim Believe me, I understand.

Abdullah But my English: bounds and leaps, yes?

Jim The Khan is very impressive.

Abdullah *Sthaa Pashto sanga da?* [How is your Pashto coming?]

Jim *Laz laz.* [Bit by bit.]
    I send greetings to your family.

Abdullah And I yours.

Jim Your wife, by now she must have –

Abdullah Yes.

Jim Congratulations.

Abdullah (*with a dismissive wave*) Anh. It is nother girl. Girl and girl and girl and still only one son. Still, God give me but one gift.

Your wife, she is finally . . . ? (*He gestures a rounded belly.*)

Jim No, not yet.

Abdullah Why she fail?

Jim She hasn't failed. We just haven't –

Abdullah A wife must children. More, she must bear son. A wife not bear son, less than dust.

Jim I'll make sure and pass that on.

Abdullah Two year she not give you. Why she not – (*Realising.*) Ahhhh!

(*To his men.*) *Da Warnock mayrman wacha da!* [The wife of Warnock is barren!]

Dismay amongst the men.

Mujahid One / *Khudai ba aulad darki!* [God will give you a child!]

Mujahid Two *Khudai di wazla waka!* [May God take pity on you!]

Jim Okay, let's change the subject, shall we?

Abdullah You shame me, Warnock khana. You not give notice. Now I terrible host.

Jim The less notice, the less chance of –

Abdullah Of course. Still, you journey long here to mountains, and for you I no even have tea.

Jim Well you've always said the tea here in Pakistan isn't fit to drink.

Abdullah Ah, you remember!

(*Wagging his finger at Jim.*) Very Pashtunwali. We Pashtun, we forget nothing.

(*Leaning in.*) But, tell me true. Which tea *you* prefer? Ours, or theirs?

Jim A man should keep *some* secrets, khana.

Abdullah Ahhhh! Very, *very* Pashtunwali. For us, secret, protect.

Jim Khana.

Abdullah Man keep secret, God is pleased. This way, only He know all your heart. This way –

Jim Khana. I've come to tell you I need better results.

For two years we have been men of our word. You have been my eyes in your country. In return – (*he points to the new rifles*) I have armed you with what you asked for. But for two months you have not moved from this camp. For two months I have received no information about the ISI. Why has the Khan stopped holding up his end of our bargain?

Abdullah You no get information because ISI – (*he makes a chopping motion*) cut me off.

Jim Then put aside your pride and go re-establish / the connection.

Abdullah This not pride! They cut off because I will not be puppet! Because I fight for *my* country, not Pakistan. ISI, now, support only mujahid who do what *they* say. Try make our war *their* war. But this *our* struggle! / *Our* rebellion!

Jim Whatever you think of the ISI, whatever I think of them, they are giving their weapons to fight the Shuravi.

Abdullah Ah! Yes, yes! But *who* get their weapon? *Who* get their weapon?

He thrusts a finger at his Men.

The Men (*as one*) Hekmatyar get weapon!

Abdullah This wolf who does Pakistan bidding only! Four years of war, *still* he does not fight for our people!

Jim Then *you* get out there and fight for your people! Move from this camp and use my rifles on the Shuravi!

Saeed leaves his men and comes down to join Abdullah and Jim.

Saeed You understand nothing!

Jim Saeed, / with all due respect . . .

Saeed Everything is different now!

Jim I wish to speak to the Khan alone.

Saeed You do not trust? Two years, you still do not –

Abdullah *Saeeda, chap sa.* [Saeed, be quiet.]
   (*To Jim, gesturing to Saeed.*) He, I trust. What you say to me, you say to him.

Saeed (*to Jim*) These new Shuravi soldiers, they are not the Uzbek conscripts we have been fighting these two years. These are Russian spetsnaz.

Abdullah *Special* forces. Fierce warriors.

Saeed They kill everything that moves. Our roads, littered with corpses, birds picking flesh from bones. What are your rifles against that?

Jim (*to Abdullah*) Then join with the other commanders and merge your forces.

Abdullah I cannot do this!

Jim No, khana, you *choose* not to do this! Where is the man who has shown me courage, loyalty / and sacrifice?

37

Abdullah You not understand! / You not there!

Jim What's to understand? The Shuravi are burning your country to the ground! You will get no more weapons from me till / you get out there and fight!

Abdullah *No one can be trusted!*

Jim stares at him. All the men are still.

I not move from this place, I not join forces because, now, in Afghanistan, I not know who is trust and who is serpent.
   Now, Shuravi, they make this Najibullah leader, Afghan army. This 'Soviet' puppet, he, eyes everywhere. Spies, everywhere.

Jim Where?

Abdullah In *us*!

Jim Some of your men are / working for him?

Abdullah *Imkan na lari!* [Impossible!]
   But *other* mujahid. *Many* mujahid. So I not know which seek put knife in my back.
   Under Najibullah, Afghan army now *help* Shuravi. Fight *with* Shuravi. Now I fight my own people! Brother, kill brother! Son, kill father! This, not my country! This, darkness!

The earth shakes as tank fire is heard nearby.

Jim Damn it. They saw us.

The men scramble to pack up the guns.

Saeed (*overseeing*) *Shyan sara ra tul kai! Chi zu! Chi zu!*
   [Pack everything up! Let's go! Let's go!]

Jim (*to Abdullah*) Look, I will talk to the ISI. I will get that channel reopened so you get support against the spetsnaz.

Abdullah How will you / do this?!

Jim I don't know yet! But when I do, I want your word: you will get me information again, and take the war to the Shuravi's throat!

The men clasp hands.

Abdullah Under God's eyes! My word! Yes!

Tank fire. Closer.

(*Pointing to two of his men.*) *Thaasi! Dwara Warnock Khan buzai!* [You two! Escort Warnock khan!]

Jim Khana, I don't need your men to –

Abdullah No! You are my guest. I risk my life, life my men, protect you. This I swear.

As Abdullah turns to his men, Saeed pulls Jim aside.

Saeed Warnock saab, I must speak with you in private. It is urgent. / I need . . .

Abdullah *Saeeda! Waslay ra tuli ka!* [Saeed! Pack up the weapons now!]

Saeed scrambles back to oversee his men.
   As Jim turns to go . . .

Warnock khana.

Jim turns back to him.

God see you, here, fight with us. God see your virtue. Inshallah, soon he give you son.

Jim Inshallah.

Abdullah Now I give you what my father give me.
   (*He gestures between them.*) Man to man, father to father. When your son boy, you take him by hand. You take him to place, just you and he, and then . . . you beat

him. You beat him over and over. Do this every year, one day. Every year, different day. So he never know when blows will come.

Jim stares at him as the tank fire comes even closer.

Not beat from anger or hate, but so he fear you. If son not fear you, he not love you. I fear God, I love God. My son fear me, my son love me. What we fear, we love. Only.

SCENE SEVEN

Simon's office in Islamabad, that night, mid-scene. Simon is pouring tumblers of whisky for himself and Jim.

Jim How long were you there?

Simon About a month. Started in the Panjshir. From there, Kabul, Kandahar, then circled round, and crossed back over.

Jim God, I wish I could have gone. Just to set foot. What's it like, actually being there?

Simon Beautiful, hell – everything in between. Like everywhere else in this region, only with the largest army in the world looting everything in sight because Moscow can't be bothered to feed her own soldiers.

Jim Ah, the Russians.

Simon Indeed.

They toast and drink.

Jim (*sputtering his spirits*) Jesus. / What is this?

Simon Oh, just shut up and drink it, will you?
   (*As Jim sips.*) When I crossed back over here, I met with Hekmatyar.

(*Off Jim's look.*) *Someone* on our side needs to take his measure.

Jim So?

Simon Well, for the devil himself he's rather disappointing at first.

Jim What's he like?

Simon Bit of a fatty, really. Makes him look rather boyish. No warlord fashion sense whatsoever. Fatigues, scuffed boots, bushy beard: like an Islamist Castro.

But then you look into his eyes and they chill the blood. Day after I left him I got word he'd ordered his men to start wading through the refugee camps, killing his own people because they're not pious enough.

Christ, he's almost as savage as the Russians. Do you know what *they've* started doing?

Jim Would I need you if I did?

Simon Bayoneting children.

Jim Jesus.

Simon No more 'hearts and minds' for our dear Slavic friends. Oh, no. It's all napalm and landmines now. Corpses stacked so high the stench makes it hard to breath. And I tell you, Jim, I've had it up to here with those tea-sipping cunts back home who think the Soviets are the fucking Red Cross. As if the fate of the free fucking world didn't hinge on us drawing a line in the sand and saying: 'Here, and no further, you murdering Bolshevik bastards.'

Jim You're right, Simon.

Simon About what?

Jim Your office is a piece of shit.

Simon You should see my flat. Makes this look like Shangri-La.

(*He raises his glass.*) Here's to Maggie Thatcher and her tight fucking purse strings. May she be dragged from Downing Street, draped in a burka, and stoned.

(*They toast. As Jim drinks.*) This mission here, we're just not a priority. (*He gestures round the room.*) Clearly. No, no, have to save the resources for the *real* problems. Let's not worry about the Russians invading a country the size of France, about two million refugees starving in tents. No, no, that would be *incidental* to the Cold War. Yes, *inc*idental because these poor buggers here aren't *occ*idental. All these brown-skinned Afi-Pakis, whatever do we care about them? / We're too busy feeling guilty about past sins to worry about current ones. We're too full of our own –

Jim Simon . . . Simon . . . (*Stopping him.*) Simon!

Simon Too much?

Jim Yeah.

Simon Sorry. Bit of a habit. On one's own all the time, the mouth just fills the void.

Jim How was your time back home after that?

Simon Oh! Good, good, *very* good.
   Well, wretched actually.

Jim Things all right with, uhm, / with . . . ?

Simon Jemma.

Jim Right. / Sorry.

Simon No, she's . . . God, she's magic. Ridiculous she would even be with me. I do count my blessings. But it's just . . . the pressure. You know: propagation.

Jim Yeah. I know what you mean.

Simon So then . . . Judy's still not . . .?

Jim No, not yet.

Simon But you're still trying?

Jim If I can ever get home.

Simon Yes, well, that's the problem, isn't it? I mean, most of the time I'm here and she's there, so it's a bit hard for us to – you know. So while I'm there we're pretty much – you know – the entire time. And it *sounds* wonderful. I mean, shagging day and night, till my knob is blistered to the point of –

Jim Simon.

Simon Sorry – But after a while, when thing's don't . . . hit . . .
   Well, it's just another obligation, isn't it? Just like everything else back there. Home seems this dull, grey husk of a thing. And this, this teeming, violent shithole is . . .

Jim Life.

Simon Indeed.
   God, I ache to go home. Daily. And when I do, all I think about is here.

Jim Because we're doing something here that matters, Simon.

Simon But what if we don't win, Jim? What if all this blood adds up / to nothing?

Jim We're not here to 'win', Simon. God knows if we even can. We're here to do what's right. And *that* matters.

Simon God, I hope so.
   (*Raising his glass.*) Well, here's to dead Russians and fertile wombs. May we both beget. And please God may I have a girl.

Jim You don't want a son?

Simon Christ, no.

Jim Why not?

Simon Well, sons always turn into their fathers, don't they?

SCENE EIGHT

A ringing phone. Jim steps into a pool of light and answers it. He is in his flat in Islamabad, later that night.

Jim (*groggy*) Who is it?

Saeed steps into a pool of light as he answers.

Saeed Good evening, Warnock saab.

Jim . . . Saeed?

Saeed I must speak with you.

Jim How did you get my home number?

Saeed It is urgent. Vital.

Jim Saeed, it's two in the morning.

Saeed Forgive me, Warnock saab. This was the only time I could be alone. No one must hear what we talk about.

Jim Where are you calling from? Are you on a secure line?

Saeed Yes, I made sure of this.
Warnock saab, I need, from you.

Jim What is it? What do you need?

Saeed I must have it. You must get it. I am desperate.

Jim What? What???

44

Saeed looks around, then pulls the receiver in close.

Saeed Boom box, JVC. Model PC-RM 100. With tape-to-tape capability. This last part, very crucial.

Jim Saeed.

Saeed Also, new Duran Duran tape, 'Hungry Like the Wolf'. You know, yes? And Olivia John Newton, 'Let's Get Physical'.

Jim I'm hanging up now.

Before he can . . .

Saeed One hand washes the other.

The two men stand in their pools of light. Neither moves.

You do this for me, I will do things for you.
For this, what *I* need, I will get you what *you* need.

Jim Which is?

Saeed Information.

Jim The Khan already gives me –

Saeed He gives you some. But I will give you more. I will be your ears and eyes.

Jim stands still, listening.

Our secret, Warnock saab. You and me. Only.

SCENE NINE

Afridi's office at ISI headquarters in Islamabad, the next day, mid-scene. Afridi sits behind his desk. The same Clerk as before types vigorously. Simon is arguing with Afridi as Jim stares out the window.

Simon The Russians are handing our heads to us on a pike. Two years into this operation, we need to take stock and back the horse who's pulled ahead. Can we at least agree on that?

Jim? Are you with me here?

Jim (*to Afridi*) Is that new Jag parked out there yours, Colonel?

Afridi Yes, it is.

Jim Congratulations.

Afridi Thank you.

Jim V-8 engine?

Afridi Of course.

Jim Leather seats?

Afridi Special order.

Jim Are we talking cowhide?

Afridi If one is going to drive a Jaguar / one should go all the way.

Jim Oh, I hear you. / Absolutely.

Simon I'm sorry, would it be possible to stick to the subject?

Afridi Mr Craig, I am patiently waiting to raise the issue that I called this meeting for. So perhaps you could cut directly to your point, if you indeed have one and are not like so many Englishmen who simply love the sound of their own voice.

Clerk Oh, very nice, very good. 'A hit,' sir, 'a very palpable hit.'

Afridi Corporal.

Clerk Yes, sir?

Afridi Get out.

Clerk Yes, sir.

And he does.

Simon My point, Colonel, is we should be throwing all our resources behind Massoud. On his own, the man has just crushed the Soviets' Fortieth Army when they tried to prise him out of the Panjshir.

Afridi Massoud is a mathematician, Mr Craig. Are we to have a man who fiddles with fractions spearhead this war against the greatest army in the world?

Simon Look at what he's done with almost nothing! My God, we give this man some *real* weapons and he'll be off to the races!

Afridi Massoud's army is full of Shia. Unacceptable both to us and almost all Afghans. If you would bother to learn the difference between Sunni and Shia –

Simon I don't care if they're Lebanese Buddhists! Massoud gets results!

Afridi Hekmatyar is the leader we will continue to support, Mr Craig.

Simon Hekmatyar, Colonel, is now beheading his own people when they don't show sufficient religious zeal! Is that the sort of 'leader' / you want to support?

Afridi I hear the same rumours as you, Mr Craig, but not being English, I base my decisions on facts. And the fact is Hekmatyar is the people of Afghanistan's choice / to lead the resistance.

Simon No, Colonel, he is not! I have just been in Afghanistan, covered the bloody country, north to south, and Massoud is who / they want!

47

Afridi No.

Simon (*biting every word*) Is there *ever* a 'yes' with you? Is 'yes' even *in* your / repertoire?

Jim (*cutting him off*) Simon. Massoud is off the table.
(*Stopping Simon's protest.*) Let it go.
(*To Afridi.*) Let's hear what the colonel has to say.

Afridi (*rising to his feet*) Gentlemen, here in Pakistan things have changed. After four years of this struggle, our eyes have been opened. We see now that we are a country, Mr Craig, like your Israel.

Simon Oh, must we? Every time?

Afridi Your people survive there, they thrive, because of your bedrock.

Simon Which is what – falafel? Hummus?

Afridi God. Your faith is what sustains your people. It is what binds you together in the face of your enemies.
   Now the Russian bear grows closer and his claws graze our cheeks. So now we understand the need for such a binding. We understand that without Islam – a strict, correct Islam – Pakistan will fall.

Jim So what is it you want, Colonel?

Afridi What *I* want is unimportant, Mr Warnock. My country is what we are discussing. And what *it* needs is for us to be practical and start using every tool available.
   The entire world knows this is a just war. So let us allow it to join our struggle. In every Muslim nation, young men clamour to come here and fight for a cause greater than themselves. To be a part of a Sunni awakening. Crushing the Soviet infidels in the name of Islam: *this* must now be the focus of this war. *This* is how we will win.

(*He slaps his hands together.*) So. We will start with two hundred Saudi fighters. They will come and train with Hekmatyar, but they will need your weapons / and support.

Jim No.

This is a strategic war, not a religious one.

Afridi War is a slippery beast, Mr Warnock. Who are we to think we can steer it whichever way we wish?

Jim Let me be clear, Colonel. The CIA, my government, we want nothing to do with that.

Afridi What *you* want is unimportant, Mr Warnock. This war is in God's hands now. Where it goes, only He knows.

SCENE TEN

Jim and Simon on the street in Islamabad, moments later.

Simon Let's kill him.

Jim What?!

Simon Let's fucking kill him. Back alley, two in the head, I'll take care of it.

Jim When the hell did you become such a cowboy?

Simon Did you listen to what he said in there? 'Sunni awakening'? 'Crush / the infidel'?

Jim We don't choose who we go to bed with in this business, Simon. We're moving a million tons of ammo – monthly – now. Not one *ounce* goes over those mountains without the ISI's say-so. There is no operation without them.

Simon But let's at least get rid of Afridi! He's thick as thieves with Hekmatyar.

Jim You think his replacement will be different? Have you found anyone in the ISI who hasn't recently drunk the Islamist Kool-Aid?

Simon Then what the fuck are we doing here?!?

Jim Because what do you think would happen if we weren't? Yes, we're a lousy break mechanism, but we're a damn sight better than nothing!

Simon Well that's just wonderful! Maybe that should be your new motto: 'Central Intelligence: a damn sight better than nothing!'

Jim (*lowering his voice*) Look. We're going to fund Massoud on our own. We've already made contact.

Simon (*staring at him*) . . . You mean you're going to give him –

Jim Yeah.

Simon So what you said in there, again, was total –

Jim Yeah.

Simon Bastard! I shouldn't believe a word you say, should I?

Jim No.
   Will you facilitate?

Simon Of course. Christ, yes.
   All right. Good, good, *very* good.
   And look, let's start being practical ourselves.

Jim What do you mean?

Simon Abdullah Khan. Let's cut him off.

Jim No. He's damn good on the battlefield. Massoud's men are the only ones who fight as well as his.

Simon And we put all our weight behind Massoud.

Jim That's practical? Cutting off the one commander who's not a religious extremist?

Simon Resources, Jim! We have to start / being more effective.

Jim We need the Khan to check Hekmatyar. He knows him. They went to university together in Kabul.

Simon They all went to Kabul! Every one of these warlords! The same twenty families run everything. It's like a little turbaned House of Lords. Your man Khan is just a trigger-happy tribalist like all the rest / of them.

Jim The man is loyal! He keeps his word!

Simon Eyes on the Russians, Jim! The only reason we are here is to hold back those savages from burning another inch / of that country!

Jim I said no!

  The two men stare at each other.

Simon Fine. You're the purse strings; it's your money.
  It's just –

Jim (*sharp*) What?

Simon (*gesturing around them.*) All this . . . it *is* chess, Jim. Never good to get attached to one particular piece.
  For your own sake, don't forget that.

SCENE ELEVEN

A party at the Irish Embassy in Islamabad, that evening.
  Gromov stands in front of a faded white flag with a garish green shamrock. He holds a jug of bright green beer as he calls across the room to someone.

Gromov Yes!

(*Gestures around him.*) Wonderful!
(*He nods his head as if agreeing.*) Absolutely!

Jim enters with a jug of the same green beer and crosses to Gromov.

Jim (*calling across the room as well*) Great party, ambassador!

Gromov Happy Irish Day, ambassador!

Jim Thank you so much!

Gromov Top of the morning!

They watch the ambassador move on. Then . . .

(*To Jim.*) I never understand word that man says. Is it Irish he speaks?

Jim No, he's just got a thick accent and a lisp. And halitosis, so don't get too close. I already made that mistake tonight.

Gromov Look at him, he even *looks* like leprechaun.
(*Gesturing discreetly to someone else across the room.*) I feel sorry for his wife.

Jim That's not his wife, that's his mistress.

Gromov . . . Her?

Jim Yeah.

Gromov That babushka?

Jim Yeah.

Gromov No!

Jim Trust me.

Gromov What kind of man takes on burden of mistress and settles for woman like that?

Jim A lisping Irishman with halitosis.

Gromov (*looking around*) These détente functions.

Jim Like having your teeth pulled.

Gromov And why must they always be in the shabby little embassy of one of these shabby little 'neutral' countries?

Jim You tell me.

Gromov I despise these 'neutral' countries. They will not join your side, they will not join my side. Yet they clamour for our protection. I say, you want protection? Then – what is saying? – shit or get off the fence!

Jim Close enough.
    How's Elena?

Gromov Ah! My wife is at her wits' end.

Jim Why?

Gromov Jim, my daughter has become scientific proof that your capitalist idea of God is lie. For if there were all-knowing creator, he would not have created my Masha.

Jim That bad?

Gromov You have no idea.

Jim Is she still having the stomach pains?

Gromov (*with a dismissive wave*) No!

Jim So what's the problem?

Gromov It is . . . (*Spitting out the word.*) Boy.

Jim Ahhhh.

Gromov I see him in my mind's eye, Jim! There, with his sweet talk and tight black-market Levis. Every night, pacing floor, wondering, How far has he gone with my Masha? Fourth base? Fifth base? Sixth base?

Jim There's only four bases, Dmitri.

Gromov Not in Moscow.

Jim I'm sure she's fine.

Gromov You think? Look at her.
(*He takes out his wallet and shows Jim a photo.*) Look!

Jim That's Masha?

Gromov Yes!

Jim You are so fucked.

Gromov I know!
(*Brandishing the wallet.*) This is why men should only have sons. When you have daughter, your own sins come back to haunt you.

Gromov sees someone across the room.

(*Pointing discreetly.*) Tell me, what do you think of *that* woman? Do you find *her* attractive?

Jim I'm . . . not really . . .

Gromov Tell me.

Jim She's . . .

Gromov What?

Jim She's fine.

Gromov 'Fine'?

Jim Yeah.

Gromov I point out *my* mistress, and all you can say is 'fine'?

I know what you are thinking. You are looking at her, you are looking at me, and you are asking yourself, how can he do this? Why would he do this?

Jim Really, I'm not.

Gromov So I will answer you.

Jim Great.

Gromov It is practical relationship. She is kind to me, I am kind to her, we both pretend we care more than we do, and in her arms I ache for my Elena little bit less.
    Tell me, what does it say about man that he makes love to mistress and thinks only of wife?
    (*He looks at him.*) I am asking.

Jim Another man's soul is darkness, Dmitri.

Gromov Ah. I admire man who knows Russian proverb.
    You know so much, Jim Warnock. And yet you are still here.

Simon approaches them, tumbler in hand.

Simon (*seeing their beers*) Good God. What is that, fermented shamrock?
    (*Tinkling his glass.*) Trust me, you should switch to this. Christ, even the fucking Irish have better booze here than we do. There's just no end to the humiliation.

Gromov But humiliation is what you *should* feel, comrade Craig. This part of world, where your imperial lust led you and yours to carve borders over which blood is still being shed, what else but humiliation *could* you feel?

Simon Ah, Professor Gromov. All these years together and I still *so* enjoy your history lessons.

Gromov (*in Russian*) *Spasiba. / Vy ochen' dobry.* [Thank you. / You are very kind.]

Simon I'm sorry, I don't speak the barbarian tongue.

Terrible about your Fortieth Army and that cock-up in the Panjshir. Massoud and his men just butchered you, didn't they? Bit like your Waterloo, I expect.

Gromov I assume you refer to our glorious victory over that terrorist bandit. Comrade, do you believe what you read in your own newspapers now? Your American and British correspondents here, they write short stories. Brilliant fiction, but fiction none less.

Simon So I should read your *Pravda* then?

Gromov 'Pravda' is Russian for 'truth', comrade. It is name of our newspaper for reason.

Simon Well I'm sure *your* truth goes down very well back home, but *our* truth is a bit closer to the actual thing.

Gromov There is only *one* truth, comrade, which happens to be ours.

Simon I was just *in* the Panjshir, comrade. I *saw* what Massoud did to your army with my own eyes.

Gromov As we say in Russia, 'No one lies like eyewitness.'

Jim All right, gentlemen. I think / it's time we . . .

Simon Tell me, comrade, when your man Najibullah and his ghoulish little troglodytes are pulling out the fingernails of Afghan children and torturing their mothers in front of them so they'll accuse their fathers of things they can't even pronounce, when they're forced to pour petrol / *on* their fathers and strike the match themselves, is that part of your fucking *Pravda* too?

Jim Simon . . . Simon . . . (*Hissing him into silence.*) Simon!

The men stand still, aware that others are looking at them. Finally . . .

Gromov This is land of rumours. My advice to you, comrade: do not listen to whispers of those who tell stories for their own gain.

Gromov turns and glides away. Jim turns and stares at Simon.

Simon Right. Fine. Don't say it.

Simon and his empty glass leave as Afridi enters the party. Jim watches the Colonel cross the room, studiously ignoring him.

Jim (*stopping him*) Evening, Colonel! You're the man I came to see tonight.
(*He looks at his watch.*) Five minutes late. And I was told you'd be here at eight o'clock exactly.

Afridi And who told you this, Mr Warnock?

Jim Let's just say a little chicken and a bottle of wine can do wonders.
(*Suddenly switching.*) You wanna arm Saudi fighters, you use Saudi weapons, Saudi cash – we won't stop you. *If* you put Abdullah Khan back in your good graces and give him support against the spetsnaz. This or no deal. And what I also want, Colonel, is some moderation.

Afridi I am unclear as to what you are referring to, Mr Warnock.

Jim Everyone here saw you drive up in that Jag. Everyone here knows you can't afford that car, not on your salary. And everyone here knows where that money came from.

Afridi You have no right to speak to me / like this.

Jim I'm. Talking. Now.
You wanna skim off the top while men are dying to keep you and yours free? You can look yourself in the mirror and live with that, fine. But do not undermine my

authority here by rubbing your theft in my face. Because
I'm not here for V-8 engines and cowhide leather,
Colonel. I'm here for the Afghans. And God help you
if you get in my way.

*Afridi turns on his heels and swiftly departs as
Gromov re-enters, jug of green beer replenished.*

Gromov Jim! Come! They are beginning the horrible,
horrible Irish songs.

Jim Something's come up. Gotta go.

Gromov Oh! I almost forgot! The most hilarious thing.
I must share with you.

Jim Dmitri, I've really got to –

Gromov Listen, listen. Only one second. Believe me, it is
worth.
     Just now, I hear most ridiculous thing. When I hear, I
laugh till eyes water.

Jim Great.

Gromov I was told – Oh, I am going to laugh out loud
even saying!

Jim Dmitri. I've got to –

Gromov That you are assassinating Soviet officers.

The two men stare at each other. Neither moves.

That you are secretly distributing sniper rifles. That you
have changed the rules. Escalation.
     Tell me, is that not ridiculous?

Jim Absolutely.

Gromov Because if you have done this, if you *continued*
to do this . . . against my personal wishes, I would be
forced to retaliate. Starting with you. And that would
grieve me, Jim. Greatly.

SCENE TWELVE

The mountains of Jalalabad, near the Afghan border, four hours later, near dawn.

Saeed stands alone in the dark, one of the new sniper rifles gripped in his hands. As he sings the second stanza of the chorus to 'Hotel California' softly to himself, Jim enters unseen. Before Saeed can sing the stanza's last line . . .

Jim 'You can find me here.'

Saeed whirls around, his gun pointed at Jim. They stare at each other.

Where is he?

Saeed (*lowering his rifle*) He is not here.

Jim When will he be here?

Saeed He is not coming.

Jim stares at him.

He has sent me in his place. He says you are to deal with me as if I were he.

Jim And why would he do that, Saeed?

Saeed Because he trusts me.

Jim Because you're his right arm.

Saeed Yes.

Jim And did he plan this with you before or after you called me last night?

Saeed That has nothing to do with this! They are not connected!

Jim Saeed. Everything here is connected.
(*Biting the words.*) Where is he?

Saeed I have told you, you are to talk to me as if / I were he.

Jim Four hours. I drove. Four hours, middle of the night, because –
   (*He takes a folded slip of paper out of his pocket and holds it up.*) He asked. He wrote. 'Emergency.' 'Cannot wait.' 'You and me, only.' And yet here you are instead? What are you trying to pull, Saeed?

Saeed I am here *for* him! I am here to ask for –

Jim What? You want what?

Saeed RPG-7s! We must have these new weapons – this night – or we will / not survive!

Jim FUCK YOU.
   FOUR HOURS.
   FUCK YOU.

   They stare at each other.

You listen to me, boy.

Saeed I am not your –

Jim LISTEN TO ME.
   You tell the Khan, *che ze yawazay le hagha sara mûhmela kawum!* [I deal with him alone!]
   He wants more weapons? He comes himself. Because I just ran out of patience.

   As Jim turns to leave . . .

Saeed He has been shot. Many times.
   Spetsnaz. They have pinned us in the mountains.

   Jim stares at him.

Jim Is he –

Saeed Barely.

Jim What does he need?

Saeed He, he –

Jim Saeed! What does he need?

Saeed Morphine and, and / some –

Jim What? / And what?

Saeed Gauze. And your anti – what you / call, anti . . .

Jim Antibiotics, yes. Where is he?

Saeed Far, far. Too far for / us to . . .

Jim I'll get to him.
    Don't worry. He's going to be all right. I will make sure he is all right.

Saeed You were not to know this. Even as he lay bleeding, he told me, 'Saeed, there is no time. You must go and *only* ask for weapons.' He said, 'My one life is unimportant. You must save our men, not me, so they may live to fight another day.' But he is our leader. If we lose him we lose everything. So I wrote the note. But *only* so that –

Jim You did the right thing.

Saeed He must not know I have told you this. I broke my oath to him.

Jim Our secret. You and me.
    (*Then:*) Saeed. If he doesn't make it . . . If the Khan –

Saeed Then, inshallah, I will have vengeance.

Jim Saeed, this operation –

Saeed *I* will lead, as he would wish.

Jim The weapons I have entrusted –

Saeed Will be mine. What we do with them, who we use them on, *I* will decide.

We must prepare, Warnock saab. For here, soon, everything may be very different.

The two men stand still in the dark, staring at each other.

End of Act One.

Act Two

Washington, DC. April 1985. Two years later.
In the dark we hear the final rousing flourish of the
'Star-Spangled Banner'. The lights snap up on a giant
gleaming American flag. Before the billowing cloth stands
Abdullah, dressed in a beautifully tailored dark suit and
tie. His arms are raised high in triumph. His smile beams
as he speaks out to us in accented but now fluent English.

Abdullah Hello, America!
I bring you greetings from the land of my fathers, here
to this land of your founding fathers!

He holds up four fingers for all to see.

Four years! Four years, our fates have been twined. Our
hands, joined together into one fist that has struck blow
after blow for justice. So what a pleasure it is to finally
stand on the soil of this great and generous country. To
come before this committee, on this morning, and tell
you this: in four years, with your support, we have
eliminated seventeen thousand Shuravi. We have
destroyed ten thousand of their vehicles. Humbly, I ask
you: is this not a good return on your investment?
In Afghanistan, we fight the Shuravi until they are so
exhausted and thirsty their soldiers must drink the urine
of a camel to survive. Hear me: when you force a Russian
to drink the urine of a camel, God is smiling.
But now let me speak to you as one man. From this
one heart to all of yours.
Two years ago, when my body lay broken in the dust,
my blood staining the earth, an American saved my life.
America saved my life as you have saved my country. My

body, my country: all living, all fighting on, because of you. For this struggle, my flesh has been maimed, my life forever changed. And yet, my heart soars. And I have flown this day, come halfway round the world, to tell you why.

Victory beckons!

Now, after four long years of struggle, we are winning this war! Together, let us press on! Let us strike the Russian bear until the godless beast returns to its lair! Then – I swear to God! – we will have freedom, and democracy, and –

(*Suddenly changing his tone, and who he is talking to.*) I cannot say this! I will not say this!

> *The lights shift abruptly and we see we are in a dingy upstairs room in the United States Senate building, late morning.*
>
> *Near Abdullah stands Saeed, dressed in a flashy suit and bright tie. Across from them is Jim, in trousers and a sports coat. With him is his Aide and a Speechwriter. Between the two groups of men a doorway looms.*

Jim (*to his Aide*) Cut the flag, cut the music. We're not taking them with us.

Speechwriter But we gotta set the mood for them! We gotta inspire!

Jim We are not making a movie.

Speechwriter (*pointing to the flag*) Let me at least use the visual!

Jim And you're going to hang it how? With them already in the chamber?

Speechwriter They won't even know / I'm there!

Jim The answer is no!

As the Aide hurries to pull the banner down and fold it up . . .

Abdullah Jim, these words are breaking my teeth.

Speechwriter What's wrong with the words?

Abdullah (*to Jim*) They are choking in my mouth.

Speechwriter Because you're changing them! You're cutting, adding – just give the speech!

Saeed Your speech is an insult.

Speechwriter Excuse me?

Saeed Camel urine? Our struggle is a joke to you?

Speechwriter Don't tell me how to do my job and I won't tell you how to do yours, okay?

Saeed This is your 'job', and you call yourself a man? / Throwing words about like pebbles is the work of a man?

Speechwriter Hey! Bill Casey has no problem with my speeches, okay? Vice-President Bush has no problem –

Jim Enough!
(*To the Speechwriter.*) Jerry, button it.
Saeed, don't push me. Not today.

Aide Sir, it's almost time.

Jim I know.

Aide Mr Khan still has to be briefed on –

Jim Thank you, I know.

Abdullah (*to Jim*) My friend, the entire flight, I am memorising, practising, as you asked.
(*He repeats his big gesture and smile from the beginning of his speech. In a mocking voice.*) 'Hello, America! So generous, America! La, la, la, la, la!'

All for you. But I cannot speak this rubbish!
What kind of a man would write this rubbish?

Speechwriter Hello! Right here! Talk to me!

Abdullah looks at him for the first time.

Abdullah (*pointing to Jim*) He is a man and my brother;
you are fool and a stranger. Speak no more in my presence.

(*Back to his friend.*) Jim, you and I, we have always
been men of truth. Why are we stopping now?

Jim Abdullah, I *fought* to ensure you would be the
mujahid to speak to this committee.

Abdullah I am honoured to raise my voice for my people, /
but how can I . . .

Jim Because *you* they will listen to. *You* can reassure
them.

Now you need to go in there and put them at ease.

Saeed By lying to them?

Jim (*still to Abdullah*) They are voting tomorrow on the
funding for our entire operation in Afghanistan.

Saeed A Muslim's spoken word is law!

Jim (*turning to Saeed*) And *our* law says if he doesn't tell
them what they want to hear you get nothing!

Saeed (*to Abdullah*) *Khabari ma auzdawa!* [Enough of
this!]

(*He points to the door.*) *Chi zmuz sara / komak waki!*
[Make them understand / how to help us!]

Abdullah (*sharply*) *Wass yay / wakht na dai!* [It is not
time / for that yet!]

Jim We don't have time for this!

*A young female Congressional Staffer enters in heels
and a stylish business skirt-suit.*

Staffer Gentlemen, good morning. Mr Khan, welcome to America. Everything all right with your flight?

Abdullah Our flight was –

Staffer Good. So glad to hear it.
Senator Birch and the rest of the committee are ready for you. The senators' schedules are extremely packed so I need to bring you downstairs and take you right in.

Jim We need five more minutes.

Staffer And you are?

Jim Assigned to these gentlemen.

Staffer And that would be through?

Jim The Afghan Task Force.

Staffer And that is?

Jim (*evading*) Complicated to explain.

Staffer So are you with State?

Jim Not exactly.

Staffer (*grilling now*) Then who let you in?
Why are you here?

Abdullah He is here for me.
Five minutes. Please.

As the Staffer hesitates, Saeed steps forward.

Saeed Thank you. Very much.
(*Smiling broadly.*) I love your country. Very much.

The Staffer turns to exit. Abdullah stares at Saeed as he watches her leave. The moment she is gone . . .

Abdullah *Ma wartha gora!* [Do not look at her!]

Saeed *Na wartha goram!* [I wasn't looking!]

67

Abdullah *Ihtiyath kawa da Americanda da!* [You will be careful here in America!]

Saeed *Zuma sthargee daltha way / maa mzakee tha katal!* [My eyes were here, / on the floor!]

Jim Listen!
Abdullah, you have to stick to the script, no matter how worthless.
(*Cutting the Speechwriter off as he starts to protest.*)
Jerry, get out or I will have you killed.

The Speechwriter exits.

(*To Abdullah.*) Now the one in there to focus on, the one you have to win over – (*Pointing to his Aide.*)

Aide (*holding up a photo*) Jefferson Birch, Junior Senator, South Carolina.
He sits in the middle, usually falls asleep.

Jim Do not let him fall asleep.
He's the one you need to convince. If he votes to continue funding, everyone else has the cover they need to do the same.

Abdullah Then he must know the truth!

Jim Abdullah, they want to support your struggle. / Do not give them a reason not to.

Abdullah If I do not tell them what is really happening we are lost!

Jim Do not jeopardise everything / we have fought for!

Abdullah We are losing, Jim! *We are losing this war!*

The Staffer enters again. Abdullah looks at Saeed, who lowers his eyes.

Staffer (*sharply*) Gentlemen, the committee is waiting.

Jim I need two more minutes.

Staffer I need Mr Khan.

Jim I am on my knees. I swear to God, please.

She stares, pivots, and is gone. Jim turns to the two men.

Abdullah Jim, these new Shuravi helicopters, we have never seen weapons like this.

Saeed They fill the skies over our mountains, raining down rockets.

Abdullah All our supplies, pinned down on the Pakistan side of our border.

Saeed Nothing can come through.

Abdullah We are trading the last of our medicine and food for stolen fuel, just to keep fighting. But for how long?
This is why I have no choice. I must go in there now, this day, and tell this committee what they must give us.

Jim (*realising*) Abdullah, do not even *think* of going in there and asking for –

Saeed (*finally letting loose*) New weapons! Better weapons! To match those of the Shuravi!

Jim Saeed, we are not a candy store! You are not getting more weapons!

Abdullah I see, I see. *We* are to be left to our own devices. *We* are to be defenceless. But, meanwhile, *who* gets your best weapons?

Jim Don't say it.

Abdullah *Who* gets your best weapons?

Jim Don't you say it.

Abdullah *and* **Saeed** (*bellowing it as one*) Hekmatyar gets best weapons!

Jim Oh. My. God!

Abdullah This snivelling dog whose army fights not Russians but *us*!

Jim Four years! / Four years of this!

Abdullah His Pakistani masters orchestrate this! How can you sit across from them and not plunge a dagger in their hearts?

Jim Abdullah, we have no choice!

Saeed You are CIA, you always have choice!

Jim Saeed, stop watching our movies!

Saeed The Pakistanis are wrapping their fingers round the throat of my country! They are scheming to one day have Hekmatyar rule us as their puppet! But after all we have done for you, you stand there / and do nothing!

Jim (*finally letting loose*) And what is that, Saeed? What exactly have *you* done? Not the Khan, not your soldiers, *you.*
     Look at you! You're a 'Gucci Muj', Saeed. That's what we call men like you. Come here, put on a fancy suit, spend our money, but *what have you done*?

Saeed You are accusing? / Now you are accusing?

Abdullah Jim, there is no need for this. We three are together.

Jim (*at Saeed*) Answer me!

Saeed I give my heart and blood / and flesh!

Jim No, *I* give! *I* give, Saeed! *You* promise, but *I* give. Isn't that right? You promise me what I need, and I deliver.

70

But I get nothing in return! But I keep delivering, don't I? Because unlike you, Saeed, *I keep my fucking word*!

Saeed lunges at Jim as Abdullah holds him back.

Saeed (*hurling the words at Jim*) Dasi khabari matha ma kawa! / Ma tha pa kashata starga ma gora! [Do not insult me! / Do not stain my honour!]

Abdullah Enough!
(*To Jim.*) When you insult him, you insult me.
How can you accuse? For two years you have barely set foot on our soil!

Jim Because I work *here* now, Abdullah, remember? But I have to keep going back and forth, don't I? Flying back to Pakistan, sneaking in under the radar, risking my life, because *you* won't deal with my replacement!

Abdullah Because you cannot replace a man like you do a suit!

Jim Jacobson is a member of my team!

Abdullah He is unacceptable!

Jim I trust him!

Abdullah He called me 'dude'.

Saeed To his face! This Khan of Nuristan!

Abdullah (*imitating*) 'Hey, dude. How are you, dude?'

Jim He was being friendly!

Abdullah He was insulting my honour!

Jim He's a good man!

Saeed Who speaks no Pashto! Who calls us 'Afghani'! Two years on!

Abdullah (*to Jim*) You and I, *we* are a team! This new man, this dude-man, how could you thrust him on me? Why do you forsake me? Why do you break our bond?!

Jim Because I didn't want a KGB bullet in my brain! Because it's your war, your country, not mine!
   I have a life! Here! My life – *my wife* – needs me here! *This is my life!*

   The Staffer is back, with eyes and mouth wide open. No one moves. Then . . .

Saeed (*a wide smile*) Everything good. Sixty seconds.

   She stares at them. They stare at her. And she is gone. No one moves. Finally . . .

Jim I'm sorry.
   That was –

Abdullah There is no need. Your words will never hurt, my friend, because I know the heart that lies behind them.
   I am your guest. Forgive me for not acting as one.

Aide Sir, we've got twenty seconds.

   No one moves.

Jim Tell them what they want to hear, Abdullah.
   The truth is for us, not them.

Saeed (*quietly to Abdullah*) *Muz bayad sa walaru.* [Tell him what we must have.]

Abdullah You saved my life, Jim. I am forever in your debt. From you, I can ask nothing.
   But I go in there not for me, but for my country. So these words now, they are not from me, but from my country.
   I will give your speech, every word. But only if you give me the Stinger missiles.

72

Jim stares at him.

We know of these. We know what they can do.
Give us these missiles, Jim, and we *will* win. Together.

SCENE TWO

An office in CIA Headquarters, that afternoon.
  Walter Barnes, fifties, is behind a desk. Jim stands across from him. From outside the room we hear the muffled sounds of voices, phones and typewriters whirling away.

Barnes He knows about them?

Jim Yeah.

Barnes The Stingers?

Jim That the prototype's being tested, that they're in the pipeline: everything.

Barnes Jesus, Mary and Joseph.
  Jimmy, this gets out, it's gonna go down like a turd in a punchbowl.

Jim He won't tell anyone he knows about them.

Barnes How do you know that?

Jim I know him.

Barnes You 'know him'? What, biblically?
  God *damn* it, I hate leaks. The Luxembourg desk is supposed to have leaks, not us.
  Don't you have a man inside the Khan's operation? Does *he* know how he got the information?

Jim He's useless. Two years I've bent over backwards to get him music and pop-culture stuff, but his intel's worthless. Nothing I can't get / on my own.

Barnes Wait wait wait wait wait. Is this the guy we had to move heaven and earth for / to get him the . . .

Jim The new Tina Turner album, yeah.

Barnes This is that guy?

Jim I'm dealing with it.

A young agency Analyst has entered with a slip of paper in his hand.

Barnes Who the hell are you?

Analyst Mr Barnes, I was asked to –

Barnes Do I know you? Are you on my team?

Analyst No, sir.

Barnes Then what are you doing in my office?

Analyst I was told to give this to you. They said it was important.

Barnes You don't knock? You just walk in? Son, I don't even *know* you and you're already on my shit list.
    Who are you with?

Analyst I'm on the Russian desk, sir.

Barnes Good man.

Analyst Just like you were when you first started. I'm trying to follow in / your footsteps, sir.

Barnes That's great. So what do you have for me there?

Analyst It's an honour to meet you, Mr Barnes. Just to work on the same floor / as you do.

Barnes Son! We're running a war here, people are dying. What do you have for me?

The Analyst hands Barnes the slip of paper. He looks at it, then crumples it.

God damn it. (*To the Analyst.*) The answer is no. N, O. You tell them out there, I don't want to see one more of these today. You got that?

Analyst Yes, sir.

Barnes Can you deliver that?

Analyst Yes, sir.

The Analyst doesn't move.

Barnes Can you do it *now*?

Analyst Yes, sir.

The Analyst exits as Barnes brandishes the crumpled paper at Jim.

Barnes Every *day* now I get these. You know what this one is? Some well-connected yahoo in Wyoming has a truckload of Winchester rifles he wants me to ship to Afghanistan. Winchester rifles! Why don't we throw in some coonskin hats while we're at it?

Last week some gung-ho hoo-ha blew up a gas station in Arlington. Did you hear about this? His pickup truck was full of ammo and a round went off. Why was his truck full of ammo? He was bringing it to us! Who are these people?

I'm getting calls every day from congressmen, senators. Every one of them saying the same thing.

'Walter, it's time to win this thing! Walter, we have to surge! We have to surge, Walter!'

You know who surged, Jimmy? You know who fucking surged? Custer surged!

Jim Walter.

Barnes Not a damn one knows a thing about counter-insurgency. No *idea* how this kind of conflict works.

Jim Walter, I need you to pull Jacobson out of the field.

75

Barnes And do what with him?

Jim Stick him behind a desk in Luxembourg, put him under a rock, I don't care. Just get him out of Pakistan.

Barnes Jacobson's been our man in Peshawar for two years.

Jim Jacobson is an idiot. Every time I go back all I'm doing is putting out his fires. You have to replace him with a better operative.

Barnes Who? (*Points to the door.*) Message boy?
  I know Jacobson's sub-par. But we haven't had good intel from there since you left. Nobody with brains and experience wants to be out in the field any more. Nobody wants to drink dirty water and sleep on a mud floor.

Jim You have to have someone who's better / than that nitwit.

Barnes No, I don't. Jimmy, I'm having to replace people your age with twenty-year-olds. Half of them don't even drink! You wanna be a field officer and you don't drink? What are you going to do when you have to sit down for a cock-measuring session with the KGB? Order a glass of milk?

Jim Walter, my asset needs a better contact!

Barnes Then *you* go back. *You* be station chief again / if it's so important.

Jim I did four years, Walter! You want me to look my wife in the face – after what I've put her through – tell her I'm going *back*?

Barnes Which is exactly what every operative worth a damn says to me, so welcome to my world.
  (*Cutting him off.*) Enough! Let it go. We've got more pressing issues today. How'd your man do before the committee this morning?

Jim He was good.

Barnes 'Good'?

Jim Yeah.

Barnes You know what's 'good', Jim? Corndogs are 'good'. But nobody gives two hundred million dollars for corndogs. / All right?

Jim He was on message, Walter. As written, word for word, tears at the end. He was damn good. Happy now?

Barnes What did you have to promise your asset for flying in and giving the speech?

Jim I didn't promise him anything.

Barnes Good man.
   Now what about Birch? Any sense of which way he's leaning? The seventh floor just called, they wanna know.

Jim Birch is hard to read.

Barnes Don't I know it. He's a pokerfaced son of a bitch.

Jim We've got tonight to seal the deal. Don't worry. We'll get his vote, Walter. We'll get over this hurdle and we'll finally have enough funding to beef up this operation and run it right.

Barnes Maybe.
   (*Off Jim's look*.) It's not just about Birch any more, Jimmy. Even if we get the funding approved, we've got a higher hurdle now.

Jim What do you mean?

Barnes Some people don't want to escalate. They want to keep the funding level as is.

Jim Who?

Barnes You know I can't tell you that.

Jim That is defeatist bullshit. This is the most successful operation in the history of the Agency.

Barnes And thank you for the boilerplate.

Jim It's true.

Barnes Oh, well if it's *true*, let me just wave my wand and – oh, look! – problem solved.

Jim Walter, we are giving them just enough to get slaughtered! What kind of support is that? We have to escalate *now*.

Barnes Jim, people in this town have the attention span of a monkey and the spine of an eel. Key people are waffling. They're asking: 'Why are we still there? How long is this operation going to go on?'

Jim What are they doing on the seventh floor about this?

Barnes Fighting tooth and nail like I've never seen. Half the people at my level want to ratchet things up. They say the Stingers are key, they're going to be a game changer.

Jim They will be.

Barnes The other half says we don't have enough interests over there to justify escalation. Heads over hearts; keep things as they are now.

Jim Walter, you have to push back. You have to meet about this.

Barnes The meeting's today.

Jim When?

Barnes Soon as I'm done talking to you.

Jim . . . Why wasn't I told / about this?

Barnes Because you're not supposed to know. Principals only, no deputies. Can you imagine if word of this debate got back there? The Russians would smell blood and the Afghans would think we were stabbing them in the back.

This is just you and me. Because you've earned the right to know. Now I've got no idea which way it's going to go, but this is it. On the seventh floor, right now, everyone throws in their two cents and it gets decided. I'm speaking for you, me, and the rest of the team.

And I'm going to vote no Stingers. We stay as is.

Jim stares at him.
The Analyst re-enters the room.

Analyst I'm sorry, Mr Barnes, but there's an urgent call on line two.

Barnes Is someone in the field hurt?

Analyst No, sir.

Barnes Killed?

Analyst No, sir.

Barnes Son, unless you have a phone call for me about one of those two things, it's not urgent. Until you have something that is, do not show your face in this office again.

The Analyst exits. Jim and Barnes stare at each other.

Jim Walter, I have always been straight with you.

Barnes Yes you have.

Jim I have told you what I thought, consequences be damned.

Barnes And I have known it and I have appreciated it.

Jim You are so full of shit on this, it is pouring out of your ears.

Barnes Jim, we put Stingers in the field, there's no deniability any more. This is cutting-edge weaponry.

We might as well slap an American flag on every missile. We put these in Afghanistan, the Russians are going to up the ante.

Jim They already have. So let's do the same!

Barnes Jim! This isn't some crate of AK-47s we can afford to have fall off the back of a truck. We give Stingers to your man Khan, the other commanders, we lose control of them. These are not our people. What happens if one of them uses a Stinger to shoot down a 747 full of tourists? My God, you think the Agency would survive that?

Jim 'Primacy of trust', Walter.

Barnes Jesus, Mary / and Joseph. Spare me this will you?

Jim 'Without trust, we cannot do our job. Those who prove they can be trusted, you hold on to, at all costs.' That's what *you* taught me, / Walter! You!

Barnes Focus on the chessboard, Jimmy!
Our job there is to punish the Russians. To smack them in their Bolshevik mouths so they will think twice before ever doing this again. We've kept the Soviet Army from marching further south; we've kept Pakistan from falling apart; what more can we do there?

Jim We can *win*, Walter! Things on the ground have changed. I've seen what my asset can do. How far he will go for this. We give him – the others – what they need, they will break the Russians' will!

Barnes Jim, they are shepherds! Now God bless them and their elephant-sized balls, but *whatever* we give them – *they're* going to defeat the Soviet Army?

Jim If there is a *chance* to help the Afghans take back their country / we have to do it!

Barnes What is this mushy-headed bullshit you are dumping on my desk? The Afghans, God bless them and keep them safe, are not our problem. (*Cutting him off.*) Shut up when I am pontificating. (*Hurtling on.*) We are not there to liberate the Afghan people. We are there to keep the Soviets from winning the Cold War and tearing down / this world!

Jim *I will not stand by and do nothing, Walter! Not again!*

No one moves. Then . . .

Barnes (*in Farsi*) *Shuma digar dar Tehran nasteed.* [You're not in Tehran any more.]

Jim (*also in Farsi*) *Tehran dar qalbi men ast, Walter. Tehran hamaysha dar qalbi men ast.* [But Tehran is in me, Walter. Tehran is always in me.]

Barnes Your Farsi is still good.
    Jim. You have to let what happened in Iran go. For your sake.

Jim Do you remember Reza?

Barnes Yeah. Good man.

Jim Do you know what they did to him after we left? Khomeini's men? They held him down and made him watch his daughter be raped. Over and over. And when he closed his eyelids, they burned them off with cigarettes. Because he worked for us. And we left him. Didn't we? Because he wasn't 'our people'. Tell me, Walter. What kind of men do that?

The two men stare at each other.

Barnes 'City of Man, City of God.'
    (*Off Jim's look.*) St Augustine. Curse of a Jesuit education.

81

Every day I sit here, Jim, and I make decisions, and people die. Our side, their side; they die. And all I can be guided by is this question: Which action that I take will do the least evil in this world?

'How do I live in the City of Man while being true to the City of God?'

I'm asking.

Jim . . . I don't know.

Barnes No one does. But that doesn't stop us from trying.

In this work there is no perfect and there is no good. At best there is decency. That's the closest thing we get to winning.

The Analyst is standing in the doorway.

Analyst Mr Barnes, the caller from before, she keeps ringing.

(*Before Barnes can ask.*) She says it's urgent.

(*To Jim.*) It's your wife, sir.

The Analyst turns and leaves. Jim picks up the phone. He turns away from Barnes, his mouth close to the receiver.

Jim (*quietly*) Hi. How are . . .?

No, I *know.* I mean, are you . . .

(*He listens. Then:*) Later . . . I don't know, *late* . . . No, I have to . . . I *have* to.

(*Interrupting her.*) Look I'm in a – No! It's just that – I'm in a *very* . . .

(*Listening, then with intensity.*) I will . . . I – Listen to me – *I will* . . .

(*Then:*) . . . Me too.

Jim hangs up the phone. Finally:

Barnes I'm sorry.

Jim It's fine.

Barnes I should have –

Jim Everything's fine.

Barnes Right, good. Okay then.
(*A moment, then:*) When's Judy due?

Jim Next week.

Barnes Ah, Jimmy! You and she must just / be thrilled.

Jim We are. Thank you, Walter.

Barnes I mean, you two have been through the wringer on this.

Jim Yeah. We have.

Barnes You know . . . It never worked out for me, having a wife. I mean, I've had companionship. Women I cared for, women I paid for.
Is this getting a little too personal?

Jim Little bit, yeah.

Barnes Well suck it up.
Sacrifice. That's what this work is about, isn't it? But the thing is, Jimmy, don't sacrifice more than you need to. Trust me on this one.
(*Then, slapping his back:*) Come on! Just do what she tells you, for Pete's sake!

Jim All right, Walter, I will.

Barnes Good man! Men like us, we're built to do what we're told. That's how we work best. Am I right?

Jim You are right.

Barnes So when I come out of that meeting this afternoon, you're going to do what you're told, right?

Jim stares at him.

83

Whatever the decision is, you're going to be with me, right? You're going to do what you're told.

SCENE THREE

A hallway in CIA Headquarters, moments later.
   Jim and Simon stand in separate cones of light, phones in hand. The connection is poor so they speak louder than normal to understand each other.

Jim Hello?

Simon Jim!

Jim Simon?

Simon Can you hear me?

Jim Yes, but, it's a little –

Simon I know. Fucking lines are getting worse here, if that's even possible.

Jim Are you all right? Is everything –

Simon Twins, Jim!

Jim What?

Simon *Twins!*

Jim You mean, she had *two*?

Simon I believe that's the definition, yes!

Jim Congratulations.

Simon Thank you! Just got the call from London. Had to tell someone!

Jim Did you know you / were having twins?

Simon No! Total surprise! All of a sudden a voice from the other side of the world wakes me to tell me I'm a

84

father. Then it tells me I'm a father again. And all I'm thinking is, dear God, don't make it thrice.

Jim How is – How's, uhm, how's –

Simon For God's sake, Jim. *Jemma.* Her name / is *Jemma.*

Jim Yes, yes! Sorry! How is she?

Simon Good, good! The connection was terrible, both of us shouting down the line. Tears on my end, howling babies – plural! – on hers.

Jim How was she about the fact you weren't there?

Simon Oh, let's not ruin the moment, shall we?
But what about *you*, old man? How much longer?

Jim Due date's next week.

Simon Fantastic! I'm delirious for you in advance!

Jim Thank you.

Simon Twins, Jim.

Jim Yes, you said.

Simon Both *boys*, Jim.

Jim Ahhhh.

Simon Listen, are you alone?

Jim Yeah.

Simon Good. Now I'm hearing rumours here that you and yours are getting cold feet about escalation.

Jim Are you on a secure line?

Simon No, I'm on a string with a paper cup. Now listen. Don't go growing a wishbone where your backbone should be, James.

Jim Who have you talked to about this?

Simon No one. Yet. But if what I'm hearing is true, I will have to tell Afridi and everyone else we're in bed / with here.

Jim Simon, those are rumours, / nothing more.

Simon Jim, if you and yours don't step up – right now – the Russians are going to win. Everything we have done here will be for nothing. Oceans of blood to come. You *have* to make your people / understand this!

Jim Simon! There is no chance we are not escalating.
    I give you my word.

Simon Right. Good.
    Just had to – you know.

Jim Listen, I've got to –

Simon Right, right. Sorry to bother.

Jim No. Thank you for the call.
    And congrats again. Thank you for telling me.

Simon Funny thing is, Jim, truth be told, / just you and me . . .

Jim Simon, I really have to –

Simon I didn't even want children.
    Did it for her. How could I not?
    I mean, I'll come round. It's just the double-barrel shock of it. I mean, two of them? Do you think I could send one back? Don't they do that sort of thing round here?

Jim Simon.

Simon Still, one of them could be gay. A man can dream. Twenty years on, there'll probably be some sort of surgery. Just a painless little snip-snip / of the old . . .

Jim Simon!

Simon Sorry.

Jim hangs up the phone, turns, and walks out of his light. Simon doesn't realise he's gone and continues on.

But now they're here – or, rather, there – and I don't have the slightest idea or, God help me, the interest to . . . What kind of a man does that make me?

He waits for an answer but none comes.

Simon Jim? . . . Hello? . . . Jim?

He hangs up the phone and steps into darkness.

SCENE FOUR

A fundraiser at the Heritage Foundation, that night.
Senator Jefferson Birch, fifties, is behind a lectern, mid-speech to a room full of well-dressed, well-heeled guests. Behind him stands the female congressional Staffer we met before. Jim and Barnes stand off to the side, watching.

Birch Now I want you folks to understand something. This fundraiser tonight is not some charity ball. Tonight, ladies and gentlemen, is about asking ourselves what we truly believe. About finding out whether we have the courage to sacrifice for those beliefs, like this man!

A spotlight finds Abdullah, who blinks and waves stiffly to the guests. Just outside his light stands Saeed.

This man, here tonight, on behalf of all the brave men and women of Afghanistan. All those fearless souls, laying down their lives for God and freedom!

The guests applaud.

Because make no mistake! The plains of Afghanistan are the front lines in a worldwide struggle between communist atheism and God's community of believers. The people of the book, joined as one!

Even louder applause as Birch rouses to his finish.

So tonight, I ask you to help this man be the point of God's spear! And if you open your wallets as wide as your hearts, together, we will prevail! And as they say in Afghanistan . . .

His Staffer whispers in his ear and he doesn't miss a beat.

Soo-lam ooh-lay-kum, and God Bless America!

Rapturous applause.
The guests begin to break up and mingle as the Staffer disappears amongst them and waiters pass food and drink.
Birch has made his way through the admiring guests to Abdullah and Saeed, as Jim and Barnes follow close behind.

(*Hand extended.*) Mr Khan, put 'er there! That was a heck of a speech you gave my committee this morning. Sir, you could talk a dog off a meat truck.

Abdullah (*as they shake*) Forgive me, Senator, but is this a good thing?

Birch Is the Pope Catholic?

Abdullah and Saeed briefly confer.

Abdullah (*to Birch*) Yes, I believe he is.

Barnes Senator, that was an inspiring –

Birch (*cutting him off*) Walter, do me a favour: save your butterin' for your beans.

(*Back to Abdullah.*) Mr Khan, let's be clear. I believe every word I said up there. I'm proud to ask people like this to give you their money. But, sir, this is private money. What you want is taxpayer money. And the bar's a bit higher for that.

Now what about all this mujahid infighting I'm hearing about?

Abdullah Families quarrel, Senator. But in the end, what family does not come together in an embrace?

Birch I'm hearing that you, Massoud, Hekmatyar – y'all are spending more time shooting each other than the Russians.

Abdullah These are rumours, Senator. In war, rumours are used against you when your enemy has nothing left.

Birch Then what I need is some concrete proof those rumours are wrong.

Abdullah Tell me, Senator, when a man says you are a camel, how does one prove you are not?

Birch (*sharp*) By not being a camel, Mr Khan. That'd be a start.

Jim steps in quickly before Abdullah can respond.

Jim Senator, I think what the Khan means is –

Birch I don't believe we've met.

Jim James Warnock, sir. I work for Mr Barnes.

Birch Then let him do your talking.
(*Shifting back to Abdullah.*) What do you think of this new man running things in Moscow? You think this Gorbachev's on the level?

Abdullah We do not trust any man who sits on the Kremlin throne.

Birch Good, I agree. (*Mocking.*) 'Let's reduce our arsenals! Let's be friends!' Friends, my tush! He's a serpent in the grass, this Gorbachev.

Saeed And with a serpent you must strike its head!

Birch Absolutely, son!

Saeed Before it strikes you!

Birch That's the God's truth!

Saeed (*pouncing*) And this is why you must give us your newest weapons! So we may strike the / Russian serpent before it is too late!

Abdullah (*to Saeed*) *Chap sa! Kar ma kharapawa!* [Shut your mouth! You will ruin everything!]

Birch (*to Saeed*) Too late for what?

Abdullah You must forgive my associate. He meant nothing by this.

Birch (*still to Saeed*) What's nipping at your heels, son?

Before Saeed can speak . . .

Abdullah Unfortunately you have heard all the English he speaks. So now he must stand and be silent before he stains the honour of his people.

Birch (*to Abdullah*) Well, see, I'm a mite confused now.

Barnes Senator, I can assure you –

Birch raises his hand and Barnes stops.

Birch This morning you stood in front of my committee and said things were smooth as silk. Russians on the run. So is that the truth or not, Mr Khan?

Abdullah . . . Senator, in our struggle, we are very close to knowing if we will –

Birch Close only counts with horseshoes and hand grenades, Mr Khan.

Are you winning, or are you not?

A moment as everyone looks at Abdullah. Then . . .

Abdullah Of course.

Birch Forgive me, but that doesn't sound very –

Abdullah If my tongue is forked, may it be pulled from its root and blackened by the sun.

The two men stare at each other.

Birch Thank you for your honesty.

Now let me be honest in turn. Mr Khan, this morning you were good enough to mention our founding fathers.

Abdullah Your George Washington was a great man. He killed many British.

Birch General Washington was a great man for many reasons. Not least of which was his farewell address, the words of which echo down to this day. 'Beware of foreign entanglements.'

Abdullah What is 'foreign entanglements'?

Birch You are, Mr Khan.

Now I want you to succeed, sir. This whole town wants you to succeed. The President called me this morning himself, asked me to back you all the way.

Abdullah We are honoured by Mr Reagan's –

Birch But I don't answer to the President. I answer to the fine people of South Carolina. And one thing my people do not like is foreign entanglements.

Abdullah With respect, I ask you to see my country through our eyes, not yours.

Birch With respect, that's not my job. My people, their needs: that's my job. Every dollar you get is a dollar they don't. So I'm gonna ask you what they're gonna ask me. 'Why should I send money to the other side of the world when I'm struggling to put food on the table for my own children?'

Abdullah Senator, this war is greater than any of us. Your people must be brought to understand the political ramifications / of this struggle.

Birch Mr Khan, these are real people. You know when real people start caring about other people's politics? When other people put a gun to their head. Did you even know what the Kremlin *was* before it came knocking on your door?

Now if I'm gonna get them to agree to sacrifice for your struggle, I can't do it with politics. But I *can* do it by talking about you. What *you've* done, what *you've* sacrificed. Something true –

(*He points to his heart.*) Straight from here.

Abdullah We are not a people who boast.

Birch No, sir, not boast; tell it like it is. What this struggle has cost you personally.

Abdullah We do not say these things in public. It is shameful for us to share our pain.

Birch Mr Khan, God help us, but here all people want to do is share their pain.

Abdullah In my country this is / not acceptable.

Birch But you're in my country, Mr Khan. You've come here hat in hand, and I'm telling you, this is what you're going to have to do.

Abdullah You ask me to tell this? To unman like this? / This is what I must do?

Birch Mr Khan, I am trying to help you! / Do you not get that?

Barnes (*to Abdullah*) Look, just give us / something!

Abdullah My wife was killed by the Shuravi.
   Last month. In the night. Burning my house. And my wife.
   My children who were there, who escaped, they saw this. My daughters tell me – they cannot sleep now for telling me – she burned and burned until her bones were charred and dust. Tell your people, this is what this war has cost me. Ask them what they would do if it was their wife. Tell them: I fight on.

Silence. No one moves.

Birch (*quietly*) May Jesus have mercy on her soul. And may he fill you with his light.

Abdullah And the Prophet, you, in turn.

No one moves. Then . . .

Birch Walk with me, Mr Khan.

Birch and Abdullah move away, heads together in conversation, with Barnes and Jim close behind.
   Saeed sees the female Staffer standing alone, collecting papers off the lectern. He summons his courage and approaches.

Saeed Hello.

Staffer Hi.

He stares at her. Then . . .

Saeed . . . I am from before.

Staffer Yes. I know.

Saeed . . . I am with the Khan.

Staffer I know.

Saeed . . . From Afghanistan.

Staffer Yes, I know.

As she starts to leave, Saeed begins to recite the lyrics to 'What's Love Got to Do With It' as an ode. The Staffer stops and stares at him. Saeed's recitation builds in intensity until . . .

I'm sorry.
I'm needed. I have to go.

She steps away, then turns back.

But thank you so much for sharing your culture.

She leaves as Jim re-enters.

Jim Saeed, come on, we need to –

Saeed Warnock saab! That woman, the senator woman. She has rebuffed me. Me!

Jim Yeah, that happens here, Saeed.

Saeed I must find another woman.

Jim There're plenty of women here.
Now come on, let's –

Saeed (*looking around*) Where?

Jim Here! Any woman here!

Saeed Those are not women, these are wives. I do not need a wife, I need a woman! I need one now!
(*The idea hits him.*) Warnock saab. You get me a woman, and I will get you information. I will get you –

Jim NO!
(*Leaning in.*) The Khan wants you around, fine. But you and me? We are through. Do you understand? Do not ask me for anything ever again.

94

Saeed I see. Because you do not trust me.

Jim You're goddamn right about that.

Saeed But the Khan, the one you call your brother, *he* you trust.

Jim The Khan and I are none of / your business.

Saeed Tell me, Warnock saab, do all men here spy on their brothers, or is it only you?

Jim Fuck you. You came to me.

Saeed Yes, because I wanted your trinkets and I knew how to get them.
   I know your kind, Warnock saab. You are a man who loves secrets more than trust. You thought, 'This foolish boy, he is just like me; he will give me what I want.' You are so greedy for secrets, you thought I would betray the Khan? Betray *our* trust? How foolish does that make *you*?

Jim I will go to the Khan, Saeed. I will *tell* him –

Saeed And I will tell him of you. And then we will see who he trusts.
   Look in the mirror, Warnock saab: that is who you should be angry with, not me.
   And do you know what *we* say? 'If you do not like what you see, do not break the mirror.'
   (*Leaning in.*) 'Break your face.'

   And he is gone, as Barnes enters and crosses to Jim.

Barnes Congratulations. You're gonna be a happy man.

Jim Birch?

Barnes Yes, indeed. And everything but the kitchen sink as well.
   I just got word. We're going all-in. The Oval Office has signed off on all available means. We're gonna send

enough AK-47s and RPGs over there to arm at least a hundred thousand mujahideen.

Jim And the Stingers?

Barnes As I said, all available means.

Jim When'll they be ready?

Barnes They'll be on the ground there within a year.

Jim My asset's going to need at least –

Barnes Your asset's not on the list.

Jim What list?

Barnes The one I'm in charge of.

Jim Walter. He's going to have to get some Stingers.

Barnes I thought you said you didn't promise him anything.

Jim He delivered on Birch.

Barnes Good for him.

Jim No one's been better in the field against the Russians. He's a nationalist, for God's sake! He's our best hope for –

Barnes You're sure about that, Jim? You wanna put all your eggs in his basket? This really who you want to go out on a limb for?

Jim I trust him.
My word. My reputation. What else do you need?

The two men stare at each other.

Barnes Fine. I'll put him on the list. He'll get Stingers. But only if you go too.
(*Off Jim's look.*) Package deal, Jimmy. You believe in him that much, then you go back full-time and oversee.

Jim . . . Walter.

Barnes Things are different there now. You go back? Soviets won't touch you. You'll be free and clear.

Jim . . . My wife and I –

Barnes And I'm sure you two can work it out.
I'm sorry, but I've got no choice. This thing is about to get bigger and bigger, and I need you there. I need someone I can trust.
It's up to you, Jimmy.

Jim doesn't move as Abdullah comes and stands beside him. They both watch Barnes leave.

Abdullah What did he want, that one?

Jim Nothing. Just business.
(*Turning to look at him.*) Abdullah. I'm so . . . I'm so sorry about your wife.

Abdullah My wife is fine, Jim.
As you say, here, the truth is for us, not them.
I pray God forgives me for my blackened tongue, but I lied not for me but for my people. I am unimportant. A speck of dust. Whatever my sins, my punishment, so be it.

Jim So be it.

Abdullah My wounds, my suffering, I tell only those who I trust, who are . . . (*He points to his heart.*) With me.
I can have no more children. My flesh has been maimed, Jim. I can have no more sons now.
No one else knows. At home, to speak of this? This is not our way. The shame would be too much.
Thank you. For listening.
(*Suddenly.*) Ah! But *you*, my friend! I hear the talk. A father you will be! Jim! Why have you held this from me?

97

Jim My daughter died.
  When she was born she . . .
  Two days ago.

  Abdullah stares at him.

Abdullah (*quietly*) Jim. My heart. My heart.
  (*Then:*) She has abandoned our world for a / better
one.

Jim Don't. Just don't.

Abdullah What did you name her?

Jim I didn't see the point.

Abdullah Jim, shall we accept the good from God but
not also the evil? This war has cost us both what no man
should pay. But God makes us suffer only so our eyes
may be opened. I see now: I fight this war not for my
people, but for Him. Only through God can there be
victory.
  Grieve, but do not question. We are but men,
stumbling in the dark. Only a fool thinks he knows
where his life journeys to. All we have is our word and
our faith.

Jim I don't have faith, Abdullah. I have what I've done,
and what I've not done, and the consequences. That's all.

  *The two men stand staring at each other as the party
  around them swirls on.*

SCENE FIVE

Pakistan. September 1987. Two years later.
  *King Faisal Street in Islamabad, in front of the Great
Mosque, early morning.*
  *Pedestrians bustle to and fro as Jim and Gromov stand
on the sidewalk, mid-argument.*

Gromov Since January our Fortieth Army has fought solely to defend itself against mujahideen attacks. No offensive manoeuvres. *Not one.*

Jim You want a medal for this?

Gromov Since almost *year*, stated Soviet policy is we are withdrawing our forces.

Jim Dmitri! You're promoting Najibullah to be president of Afghanistan. Your lapdog, running things in Kabul. This is your idea / of 'withdrawing'?

Gromov We don't care any more who runs Kabul! Najibullah wants fancy new title? Fine! Let *him* go down in flames!

Jim Dmitri, I'm late for a meeting.

Gromov No one on your side is listening. Jim! Get your people in Washington to open their ears!

Jim I don't have time / for this!

Gromov (*exploding*) Thousands of people are dying!

The both stop. They look around, then pull in closer.

We can't get our soldiers out of Afghanistan because the Khan and the rest of your proxy fighters won't stop attacking. Because of your Stingers, our forces cannot defend themselves. All we are asking is let us withdraw without bloodbath. Leash your proxies!

Jim They're not poodles!

Gromov What is this schoolyard mentality? You had your humiliation in Vietnam, so we must have ours? Jim, we are leaving with tails between legs and whole world is watching. What more do you want?

Jim To see our obligation through. Help those men who have sacrificed their blood and lives / to save their country!

Gromov Such certainty! For man who has never stepped foot there!

Do you know what your 'sainted angels' are doing to our soldiers when they capture now? They are skinning them alive, Jim! Tearing off flesh with knives!

Jim The Afghans want vengeance, Dmitri. Look what your soldiers did there!

Gromov The Afghan people know we tried! We went there to be force for justice! / Our Union of Socialist Republics stands for the cause of liberation!

Jim Would you get off your high horse just once!

Are you going to look me in the eye and say – still! – that Moscow marched to Kabul for *justice*?

Gromov (*a moment, then quietly*) No.

Jim stares. Not what he expected.

(*Slowly at first but then a dam is released.*) Those senile old men hunched round Politburo table. We do not even know which of them gave order to invade. Who signed off? Who is responsible? No one knows. Suddenly, our troops were rolling and blood was flowing, because it just happened. Dinner is supposed to just happen, not war. And our 'troops'? They sent an army of boys whose faces were not even stubbled. Half sent without weapons. In coldest of winters here, not even summer jackets. And food? Cans of rancid meat from siege of Stalingrad. From 1942! This is what those old men think of our country's children!

And they *knew* it was lost! Five *years* ago they knew! Oh, but to leave without 'victory', that would not be Russian! That would be 'grievous blow to our world authority'! And now all my country, *millions* of us, we are paying price for their arrogance! Even with your Vietnam staring us in face, still we could not learn!

Because we are Russian and we learn only by suffering! Because nothing else penetrates our *stupid monkey skulls*!

Jim, as well as many other pedestrians, stare at him wide-eyed.

What?
Things are different now. Gorbachev says we are free to speak.

Jim Like *that*? I think I prefer the old you.

Gromov This is what my wife says. We are on phone, she wants to speak about our Masha, but I can't stop talking about all this. Elena yells, 'Stop caring about politics! Care about your daughter!'

Jim How *is* Masha? Is everything . . . all right with – ?

Gromov Yes, fine. The baby is almost due.

Jim That's great. Congratulations.

Gromov Thank you.

Jim Will she still not tell you who the baby's father is?

Gromov Jim! You know I have high blood pressure! / Why are you bringing this up?

Jim You're right. I'm sorry.
Look, everything's going to work out. She's got friends, she's got her mother –

Gromov But her father is here. My family is *there*, but I am *here*.

The street is empty. They are alone now.

Why did you return to be station chief again?

Jim . . . Usual reasons.

Gromov You missed the weather?
  Jim. You were home, with your wife. Why would you leave her and come back here?

Jim I made a promise to someone to see this through.

Gromov A 'promise' is more important than your wife? Are you – what is phrase? – fucking serious? Do you know how many promises I would break to be with *my* wife?
  Jim, how did you look her in face and tell her?

Jim . . . I don't know.

Gromov What does she see in you, this woman?

Jim Some questions, it's better not to ask yourself.
  (*Then:*) I'm not done making amends, Dmitri.

Gromov Ah.
  Now you sound like Russian. Now you are finally making sense.
  Tehran?

Jim Yeah.

Gromov Tell me.
  If you wish.

Jim (*a moment, then*) Everything we'd heard was wrong. The Shah wasn't going to last. And it was not going to end well. I reported, and no one listened. I yelled, and I was told to keep my mouth shut. So I did my job. The mullahs swept in, the purges began, and I left. I left everyone who'd helped me. Assets who'd risked their lives for their country, families who'd opened their homes to me, kids I played ball in the street with. Killed. Every single one.

  Neither man moves.

Gromov Jim. When a man tries to make amends, if he does not see bigger picture, matters are made worse.

Tehran is only few hundred miles from Kabul. Do you think the mullahs there are not watching us?

Jim Trust me: I will not let the Iranians come here.

Gromov The Iranians are only *part* of bigger picture, Jim. The jails of Egypt and Jordan have been cleared out. All sent here. They are not coming for vacation cruise. More and more, every day, here to wage jihad against the unbelievers. Against you and me.

Our republics that border this region, they are all Muslim. And these Islamists, they are already knocking at the door. If you break our army and we do not have strength to stop them . . . When they are done with us, who do you think will be next?

SCENE SIX

Afridi's office at the ISI in Islamabad, an hour later.
Jim and Afridi are mid-meeting as Simon rushes in.

Simon Sorry, sorry. Traffic. Vespa pile-up, goat on the loose: / God knows.

Jim We don't have a lot of time, Simon. Can you catch up?

Simon Uhm, yes. / Of course.

Jim Good.
   (*Back to Afridi.*) Now we're going to need to go in light and lethal.

Afridi Agreed. Small units. They will cross over the Amu Dar'ya river and from there begin the rocket attacks.

Jim I want no civilians targeted. Military units / and installations only.

Afridi / The fighters on the ground must be allowed to . . .

Simon I'm sorry, I'm sorry. I lied earlier, clearly. What *are* we talking about?

Afridi The Soviet Army is raiding into Pakistan. Crossing our borders. Terrorist attacks. This is their attempt at retribution. Vengeance for their Afghan disaster. Well, we are sending a message to the Kremlin: we can cross borders too.

Simon (*to Jim*) You mean we're *actually* –

Jim Hitting them on their own turf. Our boot on the Soviet Army's throat.
    We're going to need to co-ordinate intels. Can you help with this?

Simon God, yes! Absolutely! When are we going in?

Jim Two weeks.

Simon Good, good. *Very* good. Who?

Jim Local actors.

Simon Of course. Perfect sense. But exactly *who* is / going to . . .

Afridi A Muslim must strike the soft underbelly of the Soviets' outer republics because the people there *are* Muslim. Thus Hekmatyar and his army will be their liberators.

> *Simon stares as the other two men continue to each other.*

Jim We'll have supplies ready for him by the end of the week.

Afridi Mules over the Khyber Pass would be the best, I think.

Jim / That's what I'm thinking too.

Simon I'm sorry . . . I'm sorry . . . This is *Gulbuddin* Hekmatyar, yes?

Jim Simon, we don't have time / to get into this now.

Simon (*to Jim*) The Hekmatyar calling for American throats to be slit by any Afghan who can find a free knife, yes?

Afridi Is there another?

Simon Colonel Afridi –

Afridi *Brigadier* Afridi now.

Simon Well, let's have a parade. Tell me, *Brigadier*, as you add tinder to the flames here, does it ever occur to you to check with the Afghans? You know, 'Hello, Afghans! Would you mind terribly if we try and instal a maniac to rule you and then sink your country into civil war?'

Afridi The hypocrisy of your kind never ceases to amaze me, / Mr Craig.

Simon Now would that be the tea-and-crumpets 'kind' or the circumcised-falafel-eating 'kind'? Because things fall out of your mouth, Brigadier, but one never knows what they mean.

Afridi English arrogance / is why *we* here in Pakistan must heal the wounds of this region.

Simon Tea-and-crumpets it is!
But we're not talking about Pakistan, Brigadier, we're talking about *Afghanistan*.

Afridi There is no such thing as Afghanistan.

Simon My map says otherwise.

Afridi *Your* map sliced a line through Pashtunistan that cleaved a people in two! Afghanistan is *your* creation! And for a hundred years all here have suffered from your monster! But no longer! Now, Pakistan will lead! *We* will show the way forward! *We* will crush the Shia heretics in Iran and the lentil eaters of Hindustan and restore the glory / of the Caliphate!

Simon (*exploding*) Fuck you! Fuck you! Fuck you! – *God* this feels good! – Fuck you, you Islamist fuck!
    Ten years I've had to sit in this office and listen to your rot! Denigrating me and mine, as if we came here and ruled you like bloodthirsty Huns! Who gave you your judicial system? Your parliament? What the fuck have you done since we've left but soak your land in so much blood your people wish to God we were still in charge!

> *No one moves, then Jim and Afridi rise to their feet as one.*

Jim (*to Afridi*) Great meeting.

Afridi (*to Jim*) I agree.

Jim Thank you for your time.

Afridi My pleasure.

Jim I'll get the ball rolling on my end.

Afridi And I in turn.

> *They both turn and stare at Simon.*

And you, Mr Craig. Will you be rolling the ball with us?

Jim Of course he will. Simon's a team player.
    Aren't you, Simon?

SCENE SEVEN

A hallway in ISI headquarters, moments later.
  Pakistani officials weave to and fro as Simon races after Jim.

Simon Jim . . . Jim! . . .
  (*Stopping him.*) James! What the fuck are you doing?

Jim Keep your voice down.
  He was Afridi's one demand, Simon. No Hekmatyar, no operation.

Simon Hekmatyar is assassinating the other mujahid commanders.
  (*Gesturing around them.*) With *these* people's help.

Jim And I'm checking him with the Khan. Every weapon I have is going to my asset. This is for one operation only.

Simon Listen to me! This is *my* patch, Jim. I know how / things work here.

Jim 'Eyes on the Russians.' 'Fate of the free world.' 'Line in the sand.' What *you* have always said.

Simon Things have changed, Jim! There are other factors / now in play!

Jim One million, Simon. They've killed one million Afghans. We break their army, they can never do that again. Now you look me in the eye and tell me what risk is not worth taking for that?

Simon But we have to find an endgame!

Jim This *is* the endgame. Stopping the Soviets, once and for all. What our *life* has been has been about here. What we have sacrificed / *everything* for.

Simon Christ! You don't have a fucking clue!

Jim You've lost two wars here, Simon. I'd say you're the one –

Simon We do *anything* that helps Hekmatyar, we are pushing civil war. The Kabulis will fight tooth and nail before they let that seventh-century fanatic run their lives. Blood and chaos, Jim! / Do you understand that?

Jim There wouldn't be any 'blood and chaos' if you hadn't fucked this place up – you *and* the Russians – with your Imperial Great Game bullshit!

Simon (*gesturing around*) Oh, now you sound like *them*! Shall I get you a little crescent pin for your lapel? Little hajj skullcap?

Jim This is the world we live in, Simon! We didn't choose it!

Simon Some of us have children, Jim, and we want there to *be* a –

Jim Fuck you!
  Simon, don't you *ever* – FUCK YOU!

Neither man moves.
  Simon opens his mouth to speak . . . but Jim gestures to him to be silent.

I have always asked your opinion. I have always let you have your say. But we are going to do this. Because *this* is why we are here.

SCENE EIGHT

New Year's Eve, 1988. Two years later.
  A hall in the US Embassy in Islamabad, late evening.
  Simon stands before a roomful of boisterous American Embassy staffers. He speaks out to his audience. And he has been drinking.

Simon Happy New Year's Eve!

The staffers whoop and clap.

Definitely the first order of business, yes?
    Right! 'Lessons Learned.' That's the topic, marvellous topic, let's begin.
    Lesson one: the Russians can been defeated!

Cheers from the staffers.

Tonight, as the last of their soldiers leave Afghanistan, we see that Soviet aggression can be checked, the Red Army is a little light in the loafers, and the Kremlin had better watch its fucking back. / Yes? Yes? Am I right?

Applause.

Lesson two: you won!

Even louder cheers.

Spectacular operation! Hosannas all round!
    Lesson three, and this is the key one, I think: you didn't do it on your own.

Only some of the staffers applaud this time. They are all becoming a little unsure.

But somehow, as always, you've convinced yourself that you *did*. We, the rest of the free world, especially those who gave you your very language and what passes for your manners, beg to differ.
    In actual fact, the 'we' in this victory encompass a veritable smorgasbord of parties. Afghan – (*points to himself*) white man. People who have given to the point they can give no more. People who have given to the point they are now cold and rotting and for the worms. But somehow, as always, it's all about *you*.

The room is silent now.

And this would be fine if your need for us to demonstrate our gratitude was not getting worse. Genuflecting in your direction used to be enough. But then you needed us to start kissing your bottom.

A very alarmed Jim appears.

Juuuust a little peck on the bum. So you'd know we were really, *really* grateful to be protected by your glorious non-empire empire.

Jim Simon.

Simon But after this, the floodgates have opened! Bum pecking just won't do! Now you want us on all fours as you spread your cheeks before us!

Jim Simon!

Simon Now you need us to slither our grateful tongues right up your –!

Jim *Simon!*

SCENE NINE

Jim and Simon in Jim's well-appointed office in the US Embassy, moments later.

Simon I said that?

Jim Yes.

Simon To them?

Jim You did.

Simon Do you think they were listening?

Jim Simon. You were the speaker; my staff was your audience. Trust me: they were listening.

Simon Fucking Irish whiskey. Every time.

Jim What is wrong with you?

Simon Nothing. Just – you know – holiday cheer.

Jim 'Slither our grateful / tongues?'

Simon Oh, don't, don't.

Jim You *asked* me if you could address them. Do you know how many arms I had to twist to get you an audience tonight?

Simon Jim, I'm sorry. I don't know / what I was . . .

Jim You said you had a speech. 'Important things to say about a momentous / historical event.'

Simon Yes, I know. And I did. I *do*. I was *going* to give it. I just – and then it all got away and then / there was the . . .

Jim And the whiskey and the whiskey and you're drunk.
    Enough! Look, I've got to get to the airport for a meeting. But before I go, I need to tell / you something.

Simon (*suddenly registering*) Is this *your* office?

Jim Simon, I'm trying to –

Simon You fucking git!
    Unbelievable. Fourteen years! Fourteen years, and I can't even get my closet of an office repainted. You've been back here four, and you get fucking Xanadu.
    (*Rising to his feet, drink raised.*) Here's to Maggie Thatcher!

Jim Oh, Jesus.

Simon And her tight fucking purse strings. May she be dragged from Downing Street, stripped to her skivvies, and buggered, buggered, buggered!

Jim I'm going. I'll get you a car / so you don't have to drive.

Simon No, no, no! Stay! Fill me in. How's Judy?

Jim She's fine.

Simon Oh, no, no, no. 'Fine' with you is never good. Come on, tell old Simon.

Jim Fine is / fine.

Simon (*wagging his finger*) Jim, Jim, Jim.

Jim I'm going to miss my meeting.

Simon It's family! What's more important / than that?

Jim (*exasperated now*) Fine! How's life, Simon, how are the boys, how's what's-her-face?

    Simon stares at him, eyes wide.

Simon . . . 'What's-her-face'?

Jim I'm sorry. I haven't slept in –

Simon Did you just *actually* –

Jim Simon, I'm / *really* sorry.

Simon Not once! / Not fucking *once* have you ever –

Jim I didn't mean to – (*Remembering.*) Jemma!

Simon Oh, *Jemma*!

Jim Yes. / How's Jemma?

Simon You're asking about *Jemma*! I'm sorry, I thought we were talking about what's-her-face. But you're asking about my *wife*!

Jim Yes.

Simon I wouldn't know.

Jim stares at him.

She took the boys and . . .
  Wrote it in a letter actually. Which I thought,
particularly . . . Got it today. Life is full of surprises.

Jim I'm sorry.

Simon Such is the way of the world.
  Secrets. They do . . . corrode. And trust just . . .
  (*He waves it goodbye.*) Well. Thank goodness I've got
you, Jim.

Jim Simon, I'm leaving.

Simon Ah. I see.
  When?

Jim A few days. I wanted you to hear it from me.
  Someone else will be rotating in. I'll set up the meeting.

Simon Well. I'll be here, just . . . rotating myself.

Jim I need to be with my wife.

Simon Of course. Yes, yes. As you should.

Jim My work is done here. We did it. You said it in
there. We *won*.

Simon For the time being, Jim. Because if you think your
man Khan is going to be able to stop Hekmatyar from –

Jim Don't. Just don't.
  Let me have this. Please.

Simon Of course.
  Well! Good for you, job well done. Mistakes made,
blood spilled, but how else does one learn? Wisdom for
the next time.
  Is there going to *be* a next time for you, Jim?

Jim No, I think I'm done.

Simon You *think*?

Jim Yeah.

Simon But you don't know?

Jim No.

Simon Difficult, isn't it? Letting go of the calling. The lure of certainty: ever the siren call.

Jim Go back to London, Simon. You need to go home.

Simon I *am* home, James. God help me.

As Jim turns to leave . . .

'Power corrupts.'
   'Power corrupts, and absolute power / corrupts absolutely.'

Jim Yes, Simon, I know the quote.

Simon I didn't. Not till just – Well, not the end of it. You see there's another line. One that's always left off.
   'Great men are almost always bad men.'
   Funny how we missed that.

SCENE TEN

The Islamabad Airport, an hour later. Near midnight. It is bitterly cold.
   Gromov stands alone, one suitcase in hand, as Jim rushes in.

Jim Dmitri!

Gromov Jim!

Jim I thought I'd missed you.

Gromov What a surprise. Truly.

114

This New Year's Eve night, for we atheist Soviets this is our Christmas. Happy Atheist Christmas, Jim.

Jim Dmitri, now that you're no longer – that you're leaving . . . I wanted to thank you.

Gromov For what?

Jim For making sure no one on your side killed me these last four years.

Gromov Ah. (*Shrugs.*) It was nothing.

Jim I think my wife would disagree with you.

Gromov Then you two are well suited. For here, you and I have disagreed on everything.
But a friend is a friend, Jim. No matter how wrong he is.

Jim (*pointing to his luggage*) Is that all you're taking? No kitchen sink?

Gromov I wish to take nothing from this place.

Jim You must be damn happy to get out of here.

Gromov 'The happy and the powerful do not go into exile.'
I despise quoting de Tocqueville – that snivelling capitalist propagandist – but world is upside down, so what can one do?

Jim Dmitri, you're going home.

Gromov Home? Berlin Wall has fallen. Our republics clamour to secede. This is not home I recognise.

Jim You've got Elena, you've got Masha.

Gromov Masha does not . . . Both she *and* her mother . . . There is distance between us now. Not just geographic kind.

Everything I have done here, *everything*, was for them. But now, who am I? Just some stranger from far side of world.

Over the loudspeakers the flight to Moscow is announced – first in Urdu, then in English.

After tonight, we will all be gone. Najibullah will fall. Matter of weeks. Then your man, your Khan, the other 'freedom fighters', *they* will rule Afghanistan.

Jim It's their country, Dmitri, not yours.

Gromov How I wish I had learned that many years ago.
   You know, Jim, they say tragedy is comedy, plus time. But Afghanistan? It is *tragedy*, plus time.
   I loved that country. I loved those people. I believed – mind and soul – I could make difference. But what you believe and what you do so rarely converge. (*Then, suddenly.*) Oh! I have nother joke for you! Final joke. Good to leave you with.

Jim Just so I'm clear, is this going to be a ha-ha joke or another one of your Slavic let-me-put-a-stick-in-my-eye-because-life-is-not-worth-living jokes?

Gromov (*considers*) It is bit stick.

Jim Good to know.

Gromov Kabul, that great and glorious ancient city. All through this war, through all the fighting, we protected. We protected so well that even as you were killing our soldiers, you felt safe enough to keep your embassy open. But now that you have beaten us? Now that we are leaving Kabul? You feel so *un*safe that you are closing your embassy and leaving Afghanistan altogether. Tell me: is this not funny kind of victory?

Jim History will judge, Dmitri.

Gromov I fear she will not be kind to you, my friend. I know she will not be kind to me.

As Gromov turns to leave . . .

Jim Dmitri Sergeivich.
(*In Russian.*) *Poost' vy naidyote mir v etoy zhizn.*
[May you find peace in this life.]

Gromov (*in Russian in turn*) *Ee vy, moy droog. Ee vy.*
[And you, my friend. And you.]

Gromov walks towards his flight as Jim stands still, watching him go.

SCENE ELEVEN

Afghanistan. May 1991. Two years later.
The mountains near Jalalabad, afternoon.
The bright sun warms the earth and the sky is a brilliant blue. Jim stands still, a teacup in each hand. Across from him stands Abdullah, surrounded by his men. All watch Jim intently as he slowly sips tea from one cup, then the other.

Abdullah Tell me true, Jim . . . (*He points to one cup.*) Pakistan . . . (*He points to the other.*) Or Afghanistan. Which tea do you prefer?

Breaths are held. Then, with a flourish, Jim raises the tea of Afghanistan.

Jim *Dagha di chai!* [*This* is tea!]

The Men (*shouting in delight.*) *Daghasi! Daghasi!* [Wonderful! Wonderful!]

Abdullah They all begged to stop training so they can meet you. They have all heard of our exploits. You and I, against the Shuravi. You are famous to them. Do you know what they call you?

Abdullah points to his men, who shout in unison, arms rising aloft each time.

The Men RAMBO!

Jim Great.

The Men FIRST BLOOD!

Jim Okay.

The Men PART THREE!

Jim That's enough.

Abdullah (*to his men*) Wlar sai. [Leave us now.]

They file off as Jim and Abdullah look at each other.

Jim It's good to see you, my friend.

Abdullah And you. Two years pass, but you look the same.

Jim As do you.
(*He takes a long, deep breath and exhales.*) God, this feels good. Standing here. Finally.

Abdullah Was it worth the wait?

Jim (*in Pashto*) Ara daqiqa. [Every minute of it.]

Abdullah You can tell the difference, yes? It is not like in Pakistan. Here there is a softness to the soil. Like the earth is cradling your boots. (*He points.*) There should be poplars for you to see. (*Points.*) There, eucalyptus. (*Again.*) Down there, lilacs. But . . .

Jim That was before.

Abdullah Yes.

118

God never ceases to test us, Jim. For ten years we battled the Shuravi. But when we finally drove them from our land, we found only more bitterness.

Jim I thought Najibullah's government would fall the second the Russians left.

Abdullah As did I. But Najibullah remains in Kabul, for two years, now we fight against him, and blood flows like an ocean. Before, I thought my land was in darkness. But these last two years? They are pitch black.
(*Clapping his hands.*) Enough of this! (*Eagerly.*) Did you bring it?

Jim Yes.

Abdullah Come, let me see!

Jim takes out a photograph and hands it to him.

Aaaaah.
He is beautiful.

Jim Thank you.

Abdullah How old?

Jim Thirteen months.

Abdullah What did you name him?

Jim James, Jr.

Abdullah Very original.

Jim I thought so.

Abdullah stares at the photo.

Abdullah Amazing. He looks so much like you.
Tell me, is he already making you tear your hair?

Jim And then some.

Abdullah Good. That is how it should be. (*Holding up the photograph.*) He has been a long time coming, this one.

Jim Yes, he has.

Abdullah When he was born you must have cried inside with pleasure.

Jim It was . . . My wife and I, we . . .
It was something.

Abdullah That which we must wait for is the most precious.

Jim Yes, it is.

Abdullah May I keep this?

Jim Of course.

Abdullah *Manana.* [Thank you.]

Jim *Za khwash aala swam. Pa day ghoshtane mo maathu ezat ruakay.* [It is my pleasure. I am honoured you want it.]

We hear the sounds of Abdullah's men training in arms.

Your men look good. Sharp. Saeed still knows how to whip them into shape, doesn't he?
Where is that *sarkozai* [pig]? God help me, I actually want to see him.

Abdullah Saeed is dead.

Jim stares at him.

Jim . . . When?

Abdullah Six months ago.
Soldiers from this supposed Afghan Army. These traitors who serve Najibullah. They ambushed like cowards. He

was shot three times. Once in the head, once in the chest, and once . . . below. Then his throat was slit and his body was left in the street for dogs.

Jim Jesus.

Abdullah When he fell his face was turned upward. So I know he did not die in sin. This gift, God has left me.

Jim I'm sorry.

Abdullah Yes.

Neither man moves. Then, finally . . .

Jim And . . . and *your* family, my friend? Is everyone – how is *your* son?

Abdullah I have just told you.

Silence. Jim stares at him.

Jim You never said.

Abdullah You did not ask.

Jim Abdullah.
Ten years.
Everything we – Your *son*? How could you not –

Abdullah I am Pashtunwali, Jim. Only God is to know all our secrets.
(*Then:*) And Saeed, *he* held secrets. This I know. From me, he held them. But not from you. With you he spoke alone, many times. Tell me, what did you speak of?

Jim Nothing. We never . . . nothing important.

Abdullah But what you spoke of he kept from me. My friend, what could he speak of to you that he could not bring himself to say / to me?

Jim I went to him, Abdullah. I asked him things. He never came to –

Abdullah But what did he tell you that he could not / tell me?

Jim Nothing. He told me nothing. I give you my word.
   My friend . . . Forgive me, but I can't stay any longer.

Abdullah Of course. You are busy. You must be on your way.

Jim Abdullah. You know it is not safe for / me to . . .

Abdullah You are done with our struggle, and now / you move on.

Jim I kept my word! You and I. Till the end. I was *here* till the end.
   We won, Abdullah. The Soviet Union is falling apart. Now I wish Saeed . . . You have no *idea* how much I wish. But look at what we did. How many people are free because of what you, me, Saeed – what *we* did.

Abdullah Strangers on the other side of the world are 'free' and I am to be content with this? This is why my son was killed? For strangers?

Jim Abdullah, listen / to me.

Abdullah The names of my father and my father's fathers will be forgotten, and you speak to me of 'freedom'? I do not want freedom, I want what *you* have! *I want my son!*

   The two men stare at each other.

Jim Nobody knows I'm here. Being here without authorisation? I am risking my job, everything I have done. But I came because of our friendship.
   You need to know what's happening. We're taking our Stingers back.

   Abdullah stares at him.

All the ones you didn't use – and I know how many you had, Abdullah – I need them back.

Abdullah So this now is what you call friendship.

Jim Let me finish.
We're *buying* them back, and I'm in charge. Now we are nickel-and-diming the other commanders. Twisting arms, worse. But I will get you top dollar. *More* than they are worth. And I will make sure you get every penny you are promised. I will take care of you.

Abdullah And you have come all this way just to tell me this.

Jim Yes.

Abdullah Put yourself at risk by doing this.

Jim Yes.

Abdullah Thank you, my friend. I will never forget this.
But you are not getting my Stingers.

Jim stares at him.

Jim You are going to *have* to –

Abdullah Or *what*? You will do *what*?

Jim Abdullah. This is *me*.

Abdullah You ask the impossible, Jim.

Jim I will be held *personally* responsible!

Abdullah I have already sold them.

Jim . . . To who?

Abdullah The Iranians.

Jim stares, stunned.

They offered more money than you can possibly imagine. A sum I cannot even count to.

Jim Do you have any idea what they will *do* with those?!

Abdullah The business of strangers no longer interests me.
They have my Stingers and I have their money, and
now my work begins.

Najibullah and his army killed my son. I will not rest
until every single one of them has bled his life into the
earth. I have sworn to God, if Kabul itself must be razed,
if my country must be flamed, I will have vengeance.

Jim Abdullah. Listen to me. Saeed –

Abdullah Careful, my friend.

Jim He would not want this.

Abdullah How would you know? You did not even know
who he was.

Jim You don't have the men, you don't have the resources!
You can't win!

Abdullah Which is why I have joined forces. With
Hekmatyar.

Jim stares at him.

Jim Are you . . . Are you serious?

Abdullah Hekmatyar wants Najibullah dead, I want
Najibullah dead. When that is accomplished, God will
guide what happens next. But for now, our hands are
joined as one. One fist that will strike blow after blow for
justice.

*Abdullah looks outward as behind him, in silhouette,
we see a tableau of his men.*

My eyes have been opened wider, Jim. I see clearly now.
Afghanistan is a wound that must be cleansed. Only Islam
can purify us. A true Islam. Together with Hekmatyar, we
will do this. First, we will cleanse our country. And then,
we will cross oceans.

Abdullah turns and looks at Jim.

Allahu Akbar.

Behind them, the men raise their arms as one. Each holds a gun.

The Men Allahu akbar!

End of play.

Printed in the USA
CPSIA information can be obtained
at www.ICGtesting.com
LVHW091135150724
785511LV00001B/164